Recapturing Childhood

'When all the allowances have been made for exaggeration and the attractions of panic or crisis stories, we have to admit that the condition of our children and young people in the UK at the moment gives plenty of cause for real concern. There are issues around the mental health of young people, around the provision of safe and accessible leisure space for them; around parenting and how it is best learned; around how to balance the protection of children with the need to give them appropriate challenges.
Mildred Masheder has long since established herself as a commentator of rare clarity and wisdom on these matters. This new book is a powerful and straightforward challenge to us all to put our intelligence to work for the sake of our children, to recover the space they need and the care they need. It is a book that all concerned with children's welfare should be reading and engaging with.'

The Most Reverend and Right Honourable Dr Rowan Williams, Archbishop of Canterbury.

'At the heart of a good childhood is a child who is made to feel precious. But, for many reasons, parents and carers are finding it increasingly difficult to transfer feelings of preciousness and love to children. Mildred Masheder reawakens us to the immense importance of love in a child's life – and helps us navigate through the complexities of childhood today to discover practical ways in which we can help children, and by doing so, help everyone.'

Bob Reitemeier, Chief Executive, The Children's Society

Mildred Masheder MA, Ac. Dip. Ed. is a former primary teacher and lecturer in child development and multicultural studies at the University of North London and is the author of a number of books, including *Let's Cooperate, Let' s Enjoy Nature, Freedom from Bullying, Windows to Nature, Positive Childhood, Carrier's Cart to Oxford* and the play section of *Natural Childhood*. She has also produced a video on cooperative play and parachute games. She has two children and two grandchildren.

RECAPTURING CHILDHOOD

Positive Parenting in the Modern World

Mildred Masheder

GREEN PRINT

© Mildred Masheder, 2008

First published 2008 by Green Print
an imprint of
The Merlin Press
96 Monnow Street
Monmouth
NP4 0AA
Wales
www.merlinpress.co.uk

ISBN. 9781854250957

The author asserts the right to be identified as the author of this work

British Library Cataloguing in Publication Data is available from the British Library

All rights reserved. No part of this publication may be reproduced, stored in a retrieval system, or transmitted, in any form or by any means, electronic, mechanical, photocopying, recording or otherwise, without the prior permission of the publisher.

Author's photo: John Rowley

Printed in the UK by Imprint Digital

Dedication

To my wonderful family, who have given me so much support: father, mother, brother, daughters, grandson and granddaughter as well as first, second and third cousins, nephews, nieces, great nephews and great nieces and more to come……

Acknowledgements

My heartfelt thanks to all the parents, grandparents and those interested in the well-being of children who have contributed to this book and also to Judith Rowley who has done a magnificent job in typing and editing. Her advice and collaboration have been invaluable.

Contents

Foreword by Neil Hawkes		8
Introduction by Sue Palmer		11
Chapter 1	Positive Parenting in the Modern World	13
Chapter 2	The Security of a Good Family Life	16
Chapter 3	Feelings and Emotions	29
Chapter 4	"It's good to talk and to listen"	35
Chapter 5	Creative Play and the Arts	41
Chapter 6	Keeping in Touch with Nature	56
Chapter 7	Care of the Body: Exercise, Sleep, and Food	64
Chapter 8	Happy Schooling	80
Chapter 9	Positive Behaviour	93
Chapter 10	Keeping Technology Under Control	104
Chapter 11	What Values do We Choose?	115
Chapter 12	Controlling our Time	126
Chapter 13	Parent Power in Action for Children	134
Appendices		140
Bibliography		152

Foreword

Dr. Neil Hawkes, International Education Consultant

'A gem of a book that we all need to read!' That was my immediate thought when I read through this book. Sometimes, I look for a book to inspire me when I am preparing to give a talk. Recently, I was invited to give a talk in Belgium to an audience of parents about the importance of parents having positive values and modelling them to their children. My hosts had asked me to ensure that my talk would focus on recent research and give practical, relevant, information that would support adults in this increasingly challenging role. What a joy, therefore, when I realised that in reading Mildred's book I had the foundation of my talk!

Why do I think that this simple, yet profound, book should be read by parents, prospective parents and all who want children to have the best possible childhood? Nelson Mandela's words encapsulate what I believe *Recapturing Childhood* is about:

> We are all meant to shine, as children do…And as we let our own light shine, we unconsciously give other people permission to do the same. As we're liberated from our own fear, our presence automatically liberates others.

Reflecting on these wonderful words, made me realise that if we don't recapture childhood, as Mildred urges, then we are in danger of condemning countless children to a kind of imprisonment in the home – one based on consumerism and technology. My concern, which is echoed by so many parents, is that we are not allowing children to *shine* and therefore they will not develop as well-balanced, caring adults.

For me, the power of the book is that it is based on current research and includes a broad-range of parent opinion. For instance, the recent study by UNICEF 2007, on child well-being in twenty-one economically advanced countries, which showed that in terms of perception of well-being the UK came at the bottom of the list! Yet many parents know what children need to gain a sense of well-being. As one parent in the book explained:

> Children need to feel loved and safe, starting at the early stages with constant one-to-one care from a loving adult. They need a balance of loving attentions and clear boundaries with family routines, regular shared mealtimes and peaceful rituals at bedtimes.

Central to the book, is the view that children need to feel loved and that the *relationship of a loving adult* is the key to ensure that they develop holistically: someone who is able to protect the child's natural development. Mildred avoids the trap of looking for a halcyon time of childhood, but gathers all that we now know about how children develop naturally. She skilfully analyses the challenges that parents face and how these may be overcome. She cites the positive nature of caring family life, which has the power to create a stable home environment that establishes clear expectations and boundaries for behaviour. Home life, where the 'speeded up world' we live in can be slowed, giving ample time for parent/child dialogue with an emphasis on listening. Where there is a realisation that children need to experience creative play and a relationship with the natural environment. An upbringing based on an understanding that the nurturing of positive values, such as self-confidence, is the very cornerstone of a child's emotional development.

I am delighted to recommend *Recapturing Childhood* as a book that will challenge the reader to rethink how we are raising our children in our complex society. It is a book that creates pictures of childhood, based on hope and optimism: one that will inspire readers to think again so that children will indeed *shine*. May I invite you to sit, relax and absorb the following pages of brilliantly crafted writing.

Dr Neil Hawkes has successful experience as a teacher, head teacher, senior and chief education adviser. He now works as an international education consultant to governments and ministries around the world. In England he is currently an adviser to the Qualifications and Curriculum Authority (QCA) working on values-based education. He is a Director of ALIVE (Association of Living Values International). This charity works with organisations such as UNESCO to underpin education systems throughout the world with Values Education. Neil's most recent book is *How to inspire and develop values in the classroom*.

Introduction
by Sue Palmer

That's the wise thrush; he sings each song twice over,
Lest you should think he never could recapture
The first fine careless rapture!
 'Home Thoughts, from Abroad' by Robert Browning

It seems not a week goes by without alarming revelations about the effects of modern lifestyles on children's learning, behaviour and mental health. But perhaps the media's interest in the topic will at last stimulate politicians, parents and society in general to look for ways of 'detoxifying' contemporary lifestyles, and providing a 'good childhood' for the next generation.

For this, they'll need the advice of people who really understand children, and Mildred Masheder is such a one. She has been writing about positive parenting for many years, and when researching my own book *Toxic Childhood: how modern life is damaging children…and what we can do about it* hers was one of the voices of wisdom to whom I most attended. In this, her latest book, Mildred has drawn on many other wise voices – those of contemporary parents and grandparents who have, over recent years, been busy providing good childhoods for their own families.

In the past, bringing up children used to be a collaborative endeavour – parents were able to draw on the advice of their own extended families and the wider community – and this is how it should be, because 'it takes a village to raise a child'. However, in recent years of massive social, cultural and technological change, these natural support groups have faded away, and much important child-rearing knowledge has been lost with them. Today's parents urgently need helpful advice on the best ways of bringing up children in contemporary Britain, and Mildred has assembled here a 'village' of voices to provide it.

Throughout the book, however, her own clear-headed wisdom also shines through. It is informed by her long and wide experience of children – as a teacher, lecturer, researcher and author – and her infectious enthusiasm for giving every child the best possible start in life. In the invaluable community of advice she's gathered together here, Mildred Masheder deserves to be honoured above all: a most venerable Wise Woman of the Village, to whom all concerned about children's welfare should attend.

Sue Palmer, November 2007

Chapter 1
Positive Parenting in the Modern World

'I have no name:
I am but two days old.'
What shall I call thee?
'I happy am
Joy is my name.'
Sweet joy befall thee!
'Infant Joy' by William Blake

This is a book for parents who want to give their offspring the best possible childhood, challenging on every level the pervasive influence of the consumer society. There is an increasing number of parents who are determined that their children should enjoy their natural heritage of childhood and many of them have contributed to the book, describing in practical terms how they have dealt with the ever-quickening pace of life which affects everyone, adults and children alike.

Recapturing Childhood sets out the basic needs of all children, with special emphasis on the young: their emotional, physical, social, spiritual and cognitive development. These needs are being undermined on every level and it is when we consider the whole life of present-day children that we realise how much they are missing out on every count.

This book is an exploration of how parents can still cater for their children's basic needs, which are universal. This is why I have drawn on parents' and grandparents' experiences and ideas on how they are dealing with the new problems that arise from the immense changes that have taken place in the last decades. These are volunteers from many sources sharing their contributions at the end of each chapter.

The overall picture is one of love and therefore imparting a sense of security to their children, concentrating on the whole child. Every parent wants their children to be happy and this sentiment can be at the heart of the general ethos of society, but the interpretation of what causes happiness varies greatly: some parents might be overly ambitious for their children; others might put material possessions high on the agenda. It would seem that the best thing that we can do for them is to provide an environment of full support, so that their natural tendencies can be nourished and sustained. The aim is to preserve a balance between their needs so that a rounded picture of the whole personality is achieved.

It is when we see that so much of the child's natural development is at risk that there is real cause for alarm. If we examine which areas of children's natural development are being seriously undermined, we can suggest remedies to rectify the situation. In this context, it is relevant to examine the recent study by UNICEF (2007) on child well-being in twenty-one economically advanced countries. In the six different areas studied – material well-being, health and safety, educational well-being, family and peer relationships, behaviour and the young people's perception of their well-being – the UK came bottom of the list. Especially shocking was the relationship that children and adolescents had with their family and their peers: only 40 per cent of children of eleven, thirteen and fifteen found their peers 'kind and helpful'.

So why are British children failing on all these counts? Is it too much screen-based entertainment with a consequent lack of exercise and fresh air, let alone any opportunities to take risks; also concern about 'stranger danger' and increased traffic that prevents children from venturing further afield? Is it too much junk food with possibly harmful additives? Is it an education system starting formal 'basics' too soon, missing out on early, free unstructured play and then a schooling riddled with tests and exams? Does invasive consumer pressure play a part with the endless promotion of commercialised toys and a plethora of the very latest electronic devices?

It is probably a bit of everything in a hurried and often stressful environment with parents struggling to cope. So in the following chapters we will endeavour to strike a balance between catering for children's basic needs and the challenge of a rapidly changing society.

Chapter 2
The Security of a Good Family Life

'All you need is love'
The Beatles

As soon as there are children, there is a family and, in spite of all the ups and downs, having children is the greatest joy imaginable. Families come in all shapes and sizes but the need for a secure and loving family life is still paramount for all children. There may be many adjustments that they have to make: separation, divorce, step-fathers, step-mothers, step-brothers and step-sisters, but if they can feel secure in the love that is bestowed on them, it will make all the difference.

In the speeded-up world of today, parents can be severely challenged in making time to reassure their children of their unconditional love. When planning to start a family, there is inevitably the question of whether one parent, usually the mother, should give up work and stay at home, at least during the formative years. This is quite a momentous decision to make and it is a conflict that has come to stay. Many women will not easily relinquish the hard-won right to play their part in the economy and the parents in my survey have wrestled endlessly with their decision whether or not to be a 'homemaker', at least until their child goes to a nursery at two to three years old, preferably three.

In some cases, the desperate need for an income has to take precedence and this has been greatly encouraged by government subsidies of as much as 80 per cent towards nursery day-care.

From the government's viewpoint, the economy is profiting widely from the female workforce. If there were equally generous allowances for young mothers to stay at home, it could be revealing.

It is interesting that Sure Start, launched in the late 1990s, sought to close the gap between disadvantaged and advantaged kids by spending £21 billion to provide day nurseries open from 7.30am to 6pm in deprived areas. The results of this initiative have so far proved disappointing. A Durham University study in 2007 found that the cognitive abilities of 35,000 four and five year-olds had not risen, nor had the gap in achievement narrowed between children from poorer families and those from more affluent ones. A follow-up study will be issued at the end of the year. Meanwhile, the government is allocating another £4 billion for the next three years. Again, one wonders if the results would have been of a different order it the money had been allocated to mothers who wanted to stay at home.

There is a considerable amount of recent research on the question of family or nursery care for the very young and there appears to be general agreement that very young children do better in the family home than attending nursery. In Penelope Leach's book *Your Baby and Child*, her research shows that babies and toddlers in day-care had high levels of aggression and were more inclined to become withdrawn, compliant and sad. High levels of group care before the age of three (and particularly before the age of two) are associated with higher levels of anti-social behaviour at age three. The social and emotional development of children cared for by someone other than their mothers was definitely less good.

When it might just be possible for one parent to stay at home looking after the baby and then the toddler, parents can weigh up the pros and cons; the plus side for the parent is having the time to be with their children and watch them unfold; to play with them in a leisurely way; to share household chores at a snail's pace and to explore the great outdoors; in short, bonding with them. This is the young child's natural life; they are working at understanding the world around them during all of their waking hours. There are many other advantages which will emerge.

An in-depth study in the United States by the National Institute of Child Health and Development (2004) found that three times as many children had noticeable behaviour problems in the group having over thirty hours of day-care a week while only 6 per cent had these problems in the under ten hours per week group. These problems included 'disobedience, being defiant, talking back to staff, getting into fights, showing cruelty, bullying or meanness to others, physically attacking other people, being explosive and showing unpredictable behaviour'.

A five year study by The American Association for the Advancement of Science (February 2006) showed that a loving family can boost children's intelligence. It also showed that depriving children of a loving family environment causes lasting damage to their intelligence, emotional well-being and physical stature. This confirms the findings of an earlier five-year study by the Bucharest Early Intervention Project, which recorded the well-being of children in a Romanian Orphanage from an early age and the changes they experienced when transferred to foster care. They went through amazing growth spurts, five times faster than normal, catching up after just over a year and a half. Similarly, their intelligence and their ability to express positive emotions improved greatly when they were removed into a family environment.

But staying at home is not for every parent; for some there is a contrast between a busy job and relative isolation with one or more small children that at times can be very lonely or boring. My sources of information are almost entirely parents who have finally voted to stay at home during their children's early years.

This is understandable as, although they have plenty to do, they have been able to make the time to write to me about their experiences. Some of them had, at first, gone back to work, but soon they found that the 'freedom' to do both jobs was overwhelming them and preventing them from bonding more completely with their children.

However, the decision to live on one income has been, to say the least, challenging. Some found jobs in cheaper areas, often in the country, and this had a double benefit; spending less money on housing and enabling their children to enjoy the natural world. Some could work at home taking advantage of new technology, which could lead to a simpler lifestyle and more opportunity to develop new social contacts as a parent. Both in rural and urban areas, it is easier to reach out to others when children are the initial focus: encounters at the supermarket, in the street, the play centre or the baby clinic all give a sense of neighbourhood, which often answers social needs and also paves the way for a united voice from parents demanding more action from politicians to cater for childhood's basic needs.

Special mention should be made of the particular problems that boys experience on growing up in our modern society. Their rate of development in language and literacy is in general two years behind that of girls until later adolescence. This can penalise them in a structure geared to literacy targets and the fact that they can be ahead in spatial concepts is no compensation. Clinical psychologist Susan Pinker, in her recently published book *The Sexual Paradox*, illustrates the difference in hormonal patterns in males and females.

Also, the great majority of one-parent families are fatherless and boys especially need the support of a male mentor. There is plenty of evidence to show that boys who have social behaviour problems are more likely to have been brought up without a father figure. Great stress is put on the need for good father figures as models in Steve Biddulph's book, *Raising Boys*. Young boys value their father's approval over and above peer group pressure. In the event of a breakdown in the marriage, the certainty of the father's love and interest, even though he is no longer living with the family, helps mitigate the worst effects of emotional destitution on the children.

As we consider children's needs in the chapters that follow, it will become very clear that the full support of the family is fundamental in realising every child's true potential.

Parents' contributions

The following comments have been made to the author.

Always let your children know they are loved.

The most influential factor in contributing to parents' and especially mothers' feelings of low self-esteem and inadequacy is the fact that parenting is not valued in our society. If you don't go out to work, you are not doing a proper job – you don't count. When asked what they do, they are likely to say, "I'm only a housewife," although in caring for their young children, they are doing the most important job in the world. The implications are that by sending your really young child to a nursery and going to work you are handing over to the 'experts' whereas, in reality, you are the expert and not the nursery nurses and assistants who often have little training and have to cope with quite a number of children all well under five.

When becoming a parent you have to change; it is a huge challenge. My husband and I feel as though we are on the back of a chariot and our children are taking the lead. However there are times when we have to reel in the reins and direct them as necessary. It is fun and rewarding, but hard at times because we do not always have instant answers or results. But I think that love and constancy pays off.

At the very beginning of parenthood (during pregnancy) recognise that your life will change; not for a brief period during maternity leave; not just until they are at a nursery – and then on to full school days up into their teens, but, if you are lucky, for the rest of your life.

We must get government to cater for parents' needs instead of thinking of getting mothers back to work as soon as possible. The children could profit by this in that they would be less likely to be in a state of continual rush. This could all point to a healthier life and less money needed for medicines, vitamins etc.

A very important point is that so many mothers go out to work now and leave the upbringing of their children to others, either for necessity or to buy all these consumer goods. It could be argued that they therefore resort to convenience foods and buy presents as compensation for not being available themselves and because of the pressure on their time.

I have friends in various European countries such as France, Germany and Denmark that have better support for families than the UK creating a very different situation. Low cost, good-quality housing is supported, jobs are secure and retraining available for parents after two or three years' absence.

Perhaps too much emphasis of culpability has been laid at the door of mothers and too little emphasis on the context and supporting systems that the mother operates in and with. It could be that the therapeutic community's critical assessment of motherhood has produced more insecurity and anxiety in mothers rather than supporting, giving confidence, understanding and respect of their vital roles. They may well have undermined the very fabric of the family and child-rearing that they had hoped to improve. Perhaps some re-ordering and re-assessment of our perception of mothers as being 'the make or break' carers of their offspring is necessary – geared towards some very real re-evaluation of their function. Very few human beings will do for another and suffer for another in the way that mothers typically do for their children. If that does not happen then it is not necessarily the fault of mothers but possibly the fault in our society's structure, values and perceptions of motherhood.

One of my daughters, a solicitor, has two children and employed nannies from when the children were babies. She was in her thirties before she had them and had a senior position at work. The children seemed not to have suffered as far as I could tell with this arrangement, but for parents who could not afford a full-time nanny and have to rely on child-minders or nursery schools from such a young age, it must be far from easy and I wonder about the effect on the children. I think a child should have their mother there in the early stages. My daughter disagrees with this and said it is more essential for the mother to be at home when the children reach the age of twelve or so – coming into the teenage years.

Wealthy professionals are hiring 'baby planners' at about £2,500 for all the services to be planned from cots and pushchairs to short-listing suitable nannies or nurseries. Are they missing out?

I always wanted to be with my children and enjoy them right from the start and not wake up one morning and feel I'd missed their childhood and hadn't had the time to see them grow from babyhood to at least five years old.

Our dream was for our children to have at least their first five or six years living in the countryside; free space and free from pollution of any kind if at all possible.

It is good to have different generations around to influence and guide the younger ones, uncles and aunts, cousins etc.

I feel the importance of a good family life cannot be emphasised enough. This gives a child confidence so that it views the world as an unthreatening place. The world represents adventure and unpredictability, which is non-threatening to a child raised in a loving, supportive and accepting environment. It provides codes of conduct, both moral and personal within the family; an environment of loving but firm guidance; encouraging co-operation, sharing and the necessary social skills to interact with other children and adults on going to school and work.

For birthday parties we do artistic things; we decorate and paint in gold, tiaras to take home and make salt dough napkin rings, baked in the oven and also decorate and paint them.

We make a thing about picnics; not only on warm summer days but also in winter, sitting on cushions on a rug spread out in front of the fire and a great communal dish with our favourite snacks.

Sam (six and a half) and his father, draw together a great deal, play ball games, play board games and, above all, spend hours building with Lego, wood, cardboard. Sam cooks occasionally with his mother, and they read together a great deal. The family eat together about half of the time as Sam's father gets back from work as a rule just after Sam has had his evening meal. Sam gardens with his mother and 'helps' his father with the building of cupboards etc and other DIY.

On my daughter's ninth birthday, we had a party with lots of adults as well as her own friends. I pasted the best pictures I had taken on to a big board. It showed her from her mummy's tummy (which she adored) through to the month before by which time most of her friends were in the pictures too. There were screams of delight and fascinating ruminations on the nature of time and similarities amongst the adults. She could see her life's trajectory, remember specific places and particular people from its beginning and her feelings about them. Naturally too, she and everybody in them is happy, pulling faces, dancing crazily, posing serious, or she has been caught unawares – earnestly filling a bucket with sand, eating a sausage, asleep with a smile, covered by a wave of coloured silk, hugging the cat, and so on. She is seen and now really knows it.

One afternoon at tea, my daughter told me that she would really like me to give up smoking. I did – for about four weeks – and when I started again, I recalled her injunction every time I lit up. Doctor, I have one every evening except on special occasions when I allow myself two. Now, one year later, she has come to live with me (her father) and I hardly smoke at all. She is bringing me up, setting standards and doing so with loving kindness. What more can you ask of a daughter?

I carried my babies around in a pouch a lot of the time – they felt warm and snug and almost as though in the womb.

My second child was born at home and the older one was only out of the bedroom for three quarters of an hour (birth was very relaxed and very quick). While he was out of the room, another much loved adult cooked a 'birth-cake' with him which he presented to the new baby with much pride.

The thing that I and my family put first, is the development of an harmonious, constructive, helpful, joyful attitude towards life in general and a sense of belonging to a wider community, which ultimately includes all mankind, all life on earth, the planet and the universe.

Maternal deprivation is at the root of many children's problems with development and emotional literacy. Children are less 'beaten' and have less authoritarian parents than in bygone days. But maternal deprivation is still vast, just expressed differently. Obviously working mothers, stressed mothers etc. have less time to really care for their children and there is no doubt that such children are less secure. However, this is a tricky subject because mere physical presence is no measure or guarantee of a mother's genuine nurturing of her child.

I rarely hear of paternal deprivation – a huge topic largely not discussed and although there is a group now called Fathers 4 Justice who have actively campaigned for recognition, it has on the whole been reported in a sensational way without furthering the debate that this group is trying to address – the importance of fathers, not just mothers.

Be at home 100 per cent – I was at home for my child before he was two and thereafter the majority of the time. Knowing who he is, what he wants, what he likes, what he loves, what he doesn't like or even hates – both – so that he will be able to move in his life with self-belief and independence and not be prey to materialism, cults or otherwise. To quote Alice Miller, "If I allow myself to feel what pains or gladdens me, what annoys or enrages me, and why this is the case; if I know what I need and what I do not want at all costs – then I will know myself well enough to love my life and find it interesting regardless of age or social status."

The hardest thing for me as a parent with regard to letting them go – to develop, is recognising that a teacher or the child's peer group have a significant influence on your child's life.

I felt that going to nursery should be determined by the stage of the child's development. I had two daughters; they were ready to go at different ages as one was more extrovert than the other. Therefore I decided they should go when they were ready and happy to do so.

The word 'responsibility' has, within its meaning, the ability to respond. Although there are and have been many variations throughout history, our present society values the family (generally considered a married man and woman) as the best way of bringing up children, although there has been a huge growth in single parenting and state parenting in recent years. There are systems in place now that are provided by the government which until recently were provided by the mother and extended family. Argument may rage as to the merits of different systems and in this debate we must not lose sight of the child itself. Their first needs are consistency of response so that they can learn a pattern and create a habit that can be built on. They also grow best if they are tended at first by a very few loving individuals, who also learn to respond to the particular language of the child. Only by close connection can you recognise that individualised language of sound and gesture and vice versa for the infant. This can of course be provided by someone other than the parents. We can note here the recollections of children brought up by 'the nanny' in the last century and the closeness and affection many of those children felt towards them.

We must also consider the happiness of the parents as this is very important as a backdrop for the emotional development of the child. It has been a strong and growing attitude in recent years that 'just bringing up your children' is not enough to give status to women (or men) and if a parent is severely affected by a lack of self-esteem, staying at home may not create the best atmosphere for a child.

One could say the overdose of technology, television, consumerism, exams etc. is the 'fill-in' for what is missing in human relationships – and the centre where this starts for a child is the deprivation of a real relationship with its mother or significant carer. This reflects our relationship with the outer world of people – and of nature. This is, perhaps, why some children are floundering socially.

Using the analogy of food – if we can't have 'real' food, we will have a cheaper substitute but we know it will not satisfy us or make us feel good for long – and so the search begins again. The 'good old days' – of course, this has also been the case in bygone eras – I know because I had no real mother and faced and suffered the consequences of this all my life. However, this is happening now in a different way – through ignorance and belief that exam success, for instance, can replace lost love!

The old, overly-punitive discipline regarding children, e.g. smacking etc. has been eclipsed somewhat, but has not, in many cases, been replaced with genuine love and care for children. So a kind of vacuum exists, where children are more lost, unsocialised and just as angry as before – but without the punitive sanctions of old. It creates an uncomfortable impasse and a different kind of anti-social activity. This is all very complex of course!
However at heart, the speed, the technology, the exam-fetish is the substitute to make us feel we are alive; we think we are in relationship and we are making progress when the truth may be very different. In other words, children are not valued in our society (enough) because people are not valued (enough). If we are all simply producer-consumers, does it matter if we have no places of recreation or opportunities to express love and care for our children?

I feel that the most important thing is to give a child love and time and for them to grow up confident and at ease in the world and unafraid to explore; to be able to mix with all people and to have respect for elderly people.

Shirley Williams once said, when she was interviewed on 'Desert Island Discs', that as her 'luxury' she would like to take her grandchildren. She realised that the programme would not allow this. However, she is right when she used the word 'luxury'. Grandchildren are a luxury, one to be treasured, valued, nurtured with special love and care. All too often in today's world, grandparents are harnessed to bring up the grandchildren, as their parents pursue busy careers or have to work to make ends meet. This, I feel, is unfortunate and not the ideal solution for all parties concerned.

Grandparents, in an ideal world, should be an inspired refuge, where the grandchildren gain an insight into the past life of the older generation; where they also learn various skills for which the parents have no time in their busy lives. I consider myself very fortunate that I have three grandchildren and I love spending time with them. I have travelled with them without their parents; taken them on frequent visits to the zoo, to art galleries, fed the pigeons on Trafalgar Square etc.

About a year ago, I bought two pianos – one for myself, and one for them. I have had regular lessons since then, and my seven-year-old granddaughter has now started lessons as well. Initially, we started by my playing and her singing. Now that she has lessons and has made rapid progress, a slight competition has crept into our joint musical experience, when we both 'fight' over the piano, a fight she always wins as she simply pushes me off the chair. As both her parents are not avid listeners of classical music, it is a particular joy to me when she tells me that she likes this or that easy piece by Bach or Beethoven, which I have mastered to play modestly well. I hope that we will progress together and obviously she will soon be much better than me, but I look forward to joint visits to concerts etc.

We can be of great help to the parents, having a leisurely one-to-one time with the grandchildren; having time to listen to their talk in a quiet atmosphere which can be rare for them. I find that they open up to me and they get things straight.

'I have learnt that the child really is the "father of the man" and that the growing time we call childhood is a distinct period in each of our personal histories and that what happens to us during it makes us what we are.' Michael Morpurgo in the *Radio Times.*

Chapter 3
Feelings and Emotions

Your children are not your children
They are the sons and daughters of Life's longing for itself.
....
You may give them your love but not your thoughts:
For they have their own thoughts.
You may house their bodies but not their souls, for their souls dwell in the house of tomorrow,
which you cannot visit, not even in your dreams.
You may strive to be like them, but seek not to make them like you.
From *The Prophet* by Kahlil Gibran

During the last decades we have become more and more aware of the enormous importance of the role of emotional intelligence on our children's early development. As adults we know that our feelings are uppermost in influencing all of our actions and recent research on the brain reveals a clear connection between the emotions and learning, right from babyhood. It has long been known that the two halves of the brain complement each other; the left side being primarily concerned with language, numeracy and logic and the right side with a holistic approach to intuition and creativity. Now that we are aware of the key role that the emotional side of the brain plays in any learning activity beyond simply absorbing facts and, by using our imagination, intuition and creative inspiration, we are finding ways of connecting up the whole brain.

An even more revealing finding of recent brain research is the one that is particularly relevant to the value of positive thinking. There is a kind of switchboard which controls the emotions and which then determines what goes to the thinking brain. Apparently positive emotions facilitate this passage, whereas negative ones restrict it. What a boost for a positive attitude towards our children! We all know how easy it is to tell children not to do something, rather than being positive. Now we have proof that the more we affirm them, the more we can build up a rich network of connections in the brain and learning becomes easier. This attitude will certainly build up their self-image, which plays a major role in their emotional and social well-being. Even if we are not party to this research, we know instinctively that the more we acknowledge our children's good points the more secure and self-confident they will be.

What is the significance of these findings for parents and indeed teachers? It illustrates how young children know best what is good for them; they tend naturally towards playing imaginative games and creative art. We adults are the providers of a suitable environment and then should let them get on with it. They do it because they are programmed to, not for the sake of a finished result, just for the sheer joy of creating. They don't do it for praise or being better than someone else, although they are pleased when an interest is taken in their creations and will be happy to talk about them as long as they are reassured that there will be no critical judgments. Too much praise can result in the carefree spontaneity being replaced by conformity and a need to please.

So self-confidence is the cornerstone of every child's emotional development and how can we as parents ensure that they build up a secure self-concept? They certainly need support in being able to express their emotions without shame and, if we listen, they will tend to work their problems out for themselves instead of suppressing them because they feel that no one understands. It is tempting to give unsolicited advice or to take sides on their behalf, but this will be doing them a disservice – they do have to work it out for themselves, unless of course they are victims of real injustice. Our main job is to acknowledge their feelings with respect and be ready to talk it over, if they need to. In all of these situations it is good to affirm their good qualities and your belief in them.

However we also know that low self-esteem is widespread amongst children. In a study by the National Children's Bureau (2006) of 30,000 adolescents in seven countries, in four of them 10 per cent of the girls had physically harmed themselves and most of these children had very low self-esteem.

Parents can feel really frustrated when there never seems enough time to be truly aware of their children's emotional feelings. A calm atmosphere is needed, free from interruptions from the phone or television. Emotions have a habit of bursting out at inappropriate moments and, as they grow older, young children can gradually understand how, although you care, you cannot always manage a 'heart to heart' until a little later. This is why, although 'quality time' is a good idea in this busy world, it has to be interpreted flexibly; just being available – if needed – can be enough.

Parents' contributions

A friend of mine told me that her son had been diagnosed as having depression –he was only eight – and was prescribed Prozac. I was very surprised on both counts but she said that according to the European Medical Council, one in ten British children suffer from depression and prescribing anti-depressants was common.

I came across a really clear message in the papers; that without sufficient loving care, children are unlikely to fulfill their true potential. During the last ten years research showed that in the first two years of life, a baby's brain produces whole new structures when love, affection and caring firmness are received. Further, if this kind of love is not given, these areas of the brain do not develop properly. The problems presenting themselves in this generation of children are seen amongst the affluent as well as the poverty-stricken.

When my children are frightened and lonely or upset and fragile, we sometimes need to refill our tanks. I hold my child, and ask how full their tank is. Most often, fear and loneliness means an empty tank. I ask if they are ready to fill up, and when they say yes, I let them know I'm turning on the tap. We then sit and hold each other. After a few minutes I ask how full the tank is so that they can learn to feel inside how full they are. At some point, never fail, they will say their tank is full. It could be three minutes, it could be five, I have never had them need ten minutes. They then get up, feeling again a good connection with this world through love, and always fall asleep easily. It is good to learn that when we feel disconnected from hope and safety, it is when we have let our tank go dry; filling it up is as easy as letting yourself be ready to fill up again.

With my own childhood experiences, I have discovered the damage that can unintentionally be done by never talking about feelings. So with my daughter I have made a conscious effort to open discussion with her about feelings.

Be 'a vessel' for your child's emotions: able to 'contain': not allowing your own issues to cloud your emotional reaction. I find that one way of getting rid of anger and frustration is to have some music and dance together round the room.

Children need to have confidence in themselves to survive in a modern world. I felt and feel that I need to tell my children regularly that I love them and they are good at things and to try to be positive about them all the time.

Ask parents to spend one day considering the words that they have used towards their kids. Did they send out good messages? We know now that neuro-transmitters respond positively to positive messages and negatively to negative messages. So be careful about the messages you send out; they could bounce back if they are not creative ones!

I feel strongly all emotions and feelings are valid; that they should be acknowledged and taken seriously from the smallest child to the oldest adult.'

Our children today have lots of advantages yet they are reported as being more unhappy than before. Could we, as parents, encourage them in something to make them feel proud of themselves? This would certainly enhance their self-esteem.

In the case of separation or divorce, it is of utmost importance that you keep telling your children that it is not their fault and, of course, that you love them. The other point, that is usually one of the most difficult of all things to do, is to 'allow' your children to love the parent that has left. The separation is the affair of the parents and the children will be happiest if they can continue to love each parent without feeling disloyal. It is a very hard thing to do as the emotions of jealousy and anger cannot be logically restrained, but if the welfare of the children is paramount in your mind this can give a handle on the situation and lessen the emotional fallout for them. A child is, I believe, better for being able to love both parents, regardless of the parents' perception of each other's inadequacies.

At the moment Tony is having problems with a strong classmate, a boy who dares Tony to do naughty things. Tony has told his mother about this and the problem is yet to be solved. His mother and father give time for him to tell them his problems and there is a great deal of time for them all just to be together.

The bottom line I would say for a good childhood is lots of love and attention; attention that is both emotional and stimulating for their physical and mental growth.

Children need to feel loved and safe, starting at the early stages with constant one-to-one care from a loving adult. They need a balance of loving attentions and clear boundaries with family routines, regular shared mealtimes and peaceful rituals at bedtimes.

Mothers have a problem with their desire to produce security and safety but at the same time, let their child explore new situations. It is worth spending some time examining what seems to be an instinctive, habitual reaction to see whether you are being overprotective. Having your child always in sight lessens the worry a parent may have but can dampen the spirit of exploration and independence that a child needs to learn.

Give them resourcefulness to help them deal with their ups and downs. My catch phrase to my boy is "Be your own person" and compliment him when he stands up for himself. I try not to say "Don't do that". If there is any bullying, always make your children feel that the door is always open.

Chapter 4
It's Good to Talk and to Listen

'True listening is another way of bringing stillness into a relationship. When you truly listen to someone the dimension of stillness arises and becomes an essential part of the relationship.'
'Stillness Speaks' by Eckhart Tolle

As we become more aware of the enormous importance of children's emotional needs, we realise that the key factor in reacting to their feelings is through talking to them. The more we talk together, the stronger the link between the heart and the head in the functioning of the mind. Research on the brain has confirmed what we as parents have known instinctively, that when we talk to our babies from birth onwards this is good for them.

This starts from the day they are born; we coo, sing and talk to them and this affirms the baby's need for attention and love. A dialogue develops with imitation of each other's sounds and all children are natural imitators. During the very early years they make huge strides in developing their speech, progressing to the endless question stage which can try our patience to the utmost, however proud we are of their progress.

It is particularly at this point that our listening skills are called upon and it is tempting for busy parents to give offhand replies to their children's urgent questions. So often children feel that they are not listened to and so often they are right. When a sample of children was asked what they would most like to have from their parents, there was an overwhelming request to be listened to. When children are consulted they are generally quite reasonable and can gradually understand that parents have many things to attend to and cannot always be at their beck and call. It is when they feel that "They never listen to me" that children's demands can become incessant.

Everything with regard to the relationship between parents and young children is generally a matter of how much time there is and we specially need to ensure we have enough time to talk and listen to them; in fact to have a dialogue.

For working parents time to talk is especially at a premium. The National Centre for Social Research on behalf of the Relationships Foundation found that eight out of ten working fathers and more than half of working mothers work unsociable hours, reducing the time they can spend with their children. In nearly nine out of ten working families, at least one parent works unsocial hours. What could benefit this situation are the 2006 recommendations from the Women at Work Foundation which emphasises the promotion of more part-time work for parents.

Very soon parents will be talking naturally as a family, at mealtimes, before bedtime and doing things together during weekends and holidays. This will not be a regulated discussion group; it will be more likely quite passionate with strong feelings, but as long as the children are treated with due respect, they will respond in kind and will often surprise us with their commonsense approach.

The more we have talked and listened to our children, the more they will communicate with others, especially their peers. The family is obviously the mainstay of their relationships and can serve them in good stead. First-hand experiences with others, with lots of talking and listening, will forge their social development. According to recent brain research, it is now thought that success in literacy begins in the first year of a baby's life. The communication between early parent/child or full-time carer is vital in nurturing a happy and resilient child. Early successful attachment is also thought to be connected to the development of neural networks associated with rational thought, decision-making and social behaviour.

In a survey of 1,000 primary head teachers, 90 per cent were seriously worried about the lack of talk at home and too much TV. Disturbing reports on the deterioration of young children's language ability are coming from America (1990), Germany (2003) and Japan (2003). Sue Palmer, *Toxic Childhood* (2006).

Children also need rest from contacts; time not to talk and to be still. In many ways, technological innovations have opened up new communication skills: the internet has extended possibilities of talk to a wide range of participants, (sometimes too wide, so parents need to keep a very watchful eye!) Again, mobile phones can be good for keeping in touch, especially with the growing popularity of texting, but parents should resist giving them too easily and when too young, as nothing can replace personal contact.

Probably the most important factor in children's development and indeed, adults, is having good relationships and this is greatly dependent on communication skills, including body language. So it is vital that right from the start there is as much interaction between the baby, carers and siblings as possible, continuing throughout childhood. *Quote from Krishnamurti on relationships.*

Parents' contributions

It has been anecdotally suggested that the use of the outward-facing pushchair (which became popular in the 70s) rather than the traditional pram, where babies face their parents, has affected the ability of children to learn language and to read their parents' facial expressions! This may perhaps play a small part in the change that has been witnessed in the ability of children to talk and to listen experienced by teachers.

We are truly living in an age dominated by machines; even the spoken voice is being supplanted by texting on our mobiles. It may be good to talk but where is the personal debate, discourse and real dialogue, so necessary to be practiced as future democratic citizens?

Technology is getting in the way of communication. The use of text and email is interrupting the natural growth of emotional development – in the same way that Bowlby's Theory of Attachment states that failure to attach disrupts ability to learn from emotional upset – so this distant communication can result in the inability of childhood development on emotional levels of expression. There is no opportunity for emotional engagement or development if screens and phone texts are intervening mechanisms.

I visit nurseries and am horrified to see three year-olds at the computer.

Sit with children, not talking – allowing them to take the lead.

We talk to a wider range of people than ever before, whether via the internet or interactive TV or by means of a mobile, but do we talk as much as before to our children?

The internet is a huge resource. There is endless opportunity to communicate with others.

With a second child there is not only the communication with the mother and father but with the older sibling as well.

I wasn't taught the nursery rhymes and singing games when I was young so I'm learning them through CDs and we have lots of fun singing them together.

Two of the teachers at Christopher's nursery school indicated to Arvind that they sometimes have trouble understanding Chris aged three and that perhaps he should be evaluated for any developmental issues. Arvind took this to heart. I am not at all concerned about Chris's speech. He started talking in full sentences around age two and a half and is doing well in my opinion. Yes, there are words he has trouble with and sounds ('ch' as in Chris or 'sn' as in snail) but I believe he will master it over time. And time is the key factor for me. As we discussed this summer, there is too much pressure on young children to leave childhood behind too soon. Speech is an evolutionary process that children acquire at varied speeds; Christopher is in the slower lane of that process. To have him evaluated now (and worse, receive speech therapy) would put the entire, natural process into overdrive. After discussing it with me and with other people who have raised many children, Arvind is now in accord to give Christopher more time before we evaluate his speech for any delays or problem.

I think that this reflects the pressure parents and nursery schools feel for children to become more developed/skilled than their age warrants. His day at school is three hours long, five days a week. Each day he spends a minimum of 45 minutes in the playground for 'free play' and 15 minutes each morning in the classroom for 'free play' as well. The other time is spent reading stories, singing songs, cooking, creating art with scissors, paper, crayons etc., and talking to each other. Learning colours, shapes, numbers, days of the week etc., is all play-oriented and secondary to learning how to get along with each other. *Parent from New York*

Every time they ask a question, which can happen a lot when children have learnt to speak, treat this as a quality moment. i.e. "Why is the sky blue?" What kind of answer can you give to that? Try asking them first. Children can come up with some marvelous ideas. Explore it together. Admit you don't know. Show them a crystal that creates a colour spectrum and wonder at colour in general. I don't know the answer but perhaps a children's story book from another culture might give a magical answer. If you are busy, tell them it is a really interesting question and can they remember to ask you later on – but don't treat it as a silly question!

If you ask them to do something or order them to do something and they ask "Why?" don't say, "Because I told you to" or "Just do it" or "Don't ask questions" or "Don't argue!" etc. Give them a reason; spend time explaining. It actually doesn't take long and can be quicker than a harsh threat. A child that understands the reason, even if they don't like it, will usually comply – if the reason is reasonable! If they argue their point and you see the sense of it, change your mind without feeling you have lost position. They can be right – and congratulate yourself on having such a clear-thinking child. You may have made a hasty decision which did not reflect the child's or others needs or part in the equation. It is back again to that question of how much time you allow the child to develop with you. Think what a difference it makes when you know the reason for a delay, or a traffic jam, or a person who lets you know why they are going to be late. It is the same for a child.

We try to talk to our three year old wherever we go; shopping, to the doctor's, taking the dog for a walk; it takes twice as long but we have great conversations.

Chapter 5
Creative Play and the Arts

"… plays the thing"
William Shakespeare

Creative play is the way in which young children make sense of the world around them. Right from their early years they know instinctively how to explore every aspect of their development; their feelings, their talk and their walk, and their imaginative play is no exception. They certainly need an environment where they can be free and safe to play, using all their senses and their burgeoning imagination as they progress towards participation with their peers. All we have to do as parents is to provide the basics for this stage; water, air and earth and the tools to manipulate these elements; also very simple toys so that as much is left to the imagination as possible. The sheer beauty of their stretches of imagination paves the way to a creative spirit which can be a resource to draw from for the rest of their lives.

With their imaginative play and make-believe it is just as important not to interfere or even try to share in the activity unless requested to join in. Many of these activities are shrouded in secrecy and however tempting it is to peep, it is essential to respect their privacy.

Children are naturally creative: from early days they enjoy music, song, rhythm and dance; drawing and painting; making things and modelling with clay or plasticine and we can provide the support in terms of material and experiences. This is one of the main anchors for realising a good self-image and cannot be replaced by the electronic media, which has a very limited role to play in their early creativity.

Play is the passport to their contact with their peers: learning to give and take and be part of a group, at first playing alongside others, then making tentative contact and finally joining in. One of the most demanding skills is to learn how to fit into a group happily, not to try to dominate nor to withdraw. The security from a loving family will help enormously in their social interactions and give them confidence to be creative in their fantasies. Later they will naturally progress towards games and, besides the traditional ones, they will develop their own rules and permutations in their more structured play.

Probably the single most powerful factor that operates against a fully creative and imaginative childhood is the belief that the earlier a child begins formal learning the better. Marketing can even start at the baby and toddler stage with at least a video to begin learning the alphabet or word sounds! This force reaches a pitch during pre-schooling with 'play' activities specially aimed at getting a grip on the so-called basics. These adult-structured activities are not to be confused with the natural learning that is always a fun feature of their spontaneous play. Whether numbers, spoken words, letters, sounds or music, it can never be in a vacuum and this will be gradually accommodated in their store of knowledge. They will all too soon be compulsorily attending full-time school with SATs already in the anxious sights of their parents.

Young children need to be active and this is the basis of their creative play. Apart from the harm that a sedentary life will do to their physical development, the present excessive tendency to sit and watch television, play computer games or surf the internet is taking its toll on spontaneous play. It is not only taking time away from play, but also replacing their own natural, imaginative creativity with second-hand themes, often of undue violence.

Outdoor play has been hugely restricted in recent times owing to the increase in traffic, lack of suitable play areas and open spaces and especially often exaggerated fears of children being molested. If the speed limit was reduced to 20mph in built-up areas it would make the streets a lot safer for children.

According to an article entitled 'Play England' in *The Observer* (29 July 2007), only two out of ten British children play in the streets and parks close to their homes each day, compared with seven out of ten when the parents were growing up – even though campaigners have long maintained that outdoor play is essential to every child's upbringing.

These issues are raised in the chapter on care of the body and the need for exercise. Linked to these curtailments is the lack of free outdoor play in natural surroundings. With more families living in urban flats without access to a garden or nearby park, this poses a real challenge to parents. Yet this is a stage in young people's development which cannot be neglected. It is also linked to the affinity that young children have for nature, which is a sound foundation for protecting the planet.

In September 2006, a group of over one hundred professionals, academics and writers wrote to the *Daily Telegraph* expressing concern about the marked deterioration in children's mental health, research evidence supporting this case has continued to mount. *(see Appendix 4)* Compelling examples include UNICEF's alarming finding that Britain's children are amongst the unhappiest in the developed world, and the NCH's report of an explosion in children's clinically diagnosable mental health problems.

In September 2007, a year on from the first letter to the *Daily Telegraph*, original signatories were joined by other concerned colleagues in calling for a wide-ranging and informed public dialogue about the intrinsic nature and value of play in children's healthy development, and how we might ensure its place at the heart of twenty-first-century childhood. In this second letter, the following points were made:

We believe that a key factor in this disturbing trend is the marked decline over the last fifteen years in children's play.

Play – particularly outdoor, unstructured, loosely supervised play – appears to be vital to children's all-round health and wellbeing. It develops their physical coordination and control; provides opportunities for the first-hand experiences that underpin their understanding of and engagement with the world; facilitates social development (making and keeping friends, dealing with problems, working collaboratively); and cultivates creativity, imagination and emotional resilience. This includes the growth of self-reliance, independence and personal strategies for dealing with and integrating challenging or traumatic experiences.

Many features of modern life seem to have eroded children's play. They include: increases in traffic that make even residential areas unsafe for children; the ready availability of sedentary, sometimes addictive screen-based entertainment; the aggressive marketing of over-elaborate, commercialized toys (which seem to inhibit rather than stimulate creative play); parental anxiety about 'stranger danger', meaning that children are increasingly kept indoors; a test-driven school and pre-school 'curriculum' in which formal learning has substantially taken the place of free, unstructured play; and a more pervasive cultural anxiety which, when uncontained by the policy-making process, routinely contaminates the space needed for authentic play to flourish.

Parent's contributions

What children really need for healthy development is more good old-fashioned play time instead of having loaded schedules with 'get smart' videos, enrichment activities and lots of classes in a desire to help them excel. Spontaneous free play is sacrificed in the 'shuffle'.

This is a new spin on the teddy bear tea party and quite good for half-term breaks when a child complains of boredom. Choose a cuddly toy to hold a surprise birthday party for. Have the child create invitations for all the other animals and people who will attend. Choose what party games to play. Using tape, old newspaper and small items from around the house, he/she can create a pass-the-parcel (we use paper clips, hair ties, coloured pictures – things which can be put back later.) Spread a blanket out on the floor and let her/him arrange all the animals in a circle. One could make place labels at their spots. There are no end to the activities which naturally emanate from this idea and because it revolves around a birthday, I find that my daughter's enthusiasm never flags. One can never have enough birthday parties!

If you know of a dedicated musician, they may be happy to have a small child in the room as they practice (often for hours on end) and this can fascinate and produce a desire to make music later on.

My grandchildren have enjoyed all kinds of music from pop to classical right from their earliest years. Now we are all beginning to learn to play the piano. I tell them that I will be slower than them if they practice regularly as it is more difficult to learn new things when you are older.

You don't have to provide entertainment and activities for every moment of the day for your children. Children need to be left to their own devices as well as being supervised at a distance in their play.

Stimulation pressure not needed – young children are fascinated by everything in the world around them – the daily routines and the great outdoors. Every child has their own creative potential which needs to be channelled by offering the right experiences for them. Children can visit the free art galleries. When we took them to an outdoor Henry Moore exhibition we asked them "What do you think that is?"…"That's a daddy with a baby".

They are starting to take an interest in all that my husband and I do. We have a piano, synthesizers, guitars and drums at home, so they are surrounded by music.

Our children and their toys and other activities are not banished to their bedrooms as they are in many families these days. This is seen as isolating the child from the rest of the family and as treating them as second-class citizens and also cutting them off from benign adult influence. It means that there is more clutter in the communal living space but it is seen as well worth it and of benefit to adults as well as children.

I feel imaginative play and the arts are invaluable to stimulate a child's imagination. To provide the child with enormous inner reserves of creativity for their whole life, I feel providing tactile materials i.e. clay, paints, water, sand, toys, earth and taking the child to see ballet, music and theatre feeds the imagination and senses.

Children value so much more, things that you put an effort into. We helped them make a living willow structure to be a wigwam. They did not have expensive toys, making their own Waldorf dolls (out of a square of cotton).

You want to have your children running freely and being able to take risks; it should be part of their heritage, but this is a difficult one. Everything you read and hear is about danger and that feeling of security isn't there any more. If you look at it, it's not reality stuff; it's blown up in the newspapers. Still you can't help feeling that it just could happen to you. I lost my four year old in the supermarket for ten minutes – in a second they are gone and then every second that goes past is more and more terrifying. But you've got to keep it in proportion.

We don't want to keep our children cloistered indoors so we have organized a rota of parents in the street, who then keep a watchful eye on them as they escort them to local parks to play.

Children need first-hand experiences rather than virtual ones and that is the road to academic success. Their early life should be on of exploring their worlds and at the same time enjoying songs, stories and rhymes with a close adult.

We can honour and respect whatever a child creates rather than seeming to assess or judge it. Even the praise which can be fulsomely bestowed can be a mixed blessing as these are adult standards. The child can be left with a feeling that she could not manage such a success again or she can sense that this offering is not worthy of such praise. The relationship between adults and children is quite tenuous with regard to the child's creativity and reactions can be likened to an adventurous snail where the lightest touch sends it back into its shell.

When my mother leaned over me when I was painting a fabulous (in my mind) picture and said, "You've spoilt it", I was certain that I had and it was never finished. It took me many years to feel that I could paint and it did not matter what people thought about my attempts.

We could take a leaf out of the therapist's book, when interest in the work is expressed and perhaps an invitation to talk about it if they want to and say what they are expressing, rather than imposing interpretations. Very young children express themselves spontaneously rather than wanting to produce something and this is the essence of creativity.

Jasmine thought the animal masks I bought – a cat, sheep, rabbit, cow and pig – were good fun and we decided to make some fierce animals. Together we made a lion, wolf and crocodile from paper and card. Jasmine (four years) wanted to put on a show. The story she made up was that the wolf (played by me) chased the rabbit saying he wanted to catch it for its babies' dinner. Rabbit ran off to collect his friends (all played by Jasmine) – sheep, cow, pig, cat, lion and crocodile. They all confront the wolf and the wolf is frightened off declaring it is now a vegetarian!

We are now working on fairy tale characters – princesses, handsome princes and wicked stepmothers – to broaden our show repertoire!

Every child has their own creative potential which needs to be channelled by offering the right experiences for them, e.g. if Mary loves to paint, then she should be offered as many opportunities as possible for her creativity.

Although we only have a small courtyard outside, it is given over to the children, the most important item being a little homemade hut, which everyone helped to make. It is very basic, but as long as they can get in and out the rest can be left to improvisation. Indoors they make do with the kitchen table with a heavy cover over two of the sides.

We go for little walks around the block, making sure we use a passenger crossing to get them used to the routine of traffic safety rules from an early age.

I knew from the start that I didn't want my children to play with highly commercial toys and I certainly didn't see why I should fork out hard-earned cash for it either. More time spent earning money for toys we didn't need meant less time with my children. One of my earliest memories of my daughter playing is of her rocking in her bouncy chair, bashing a lovely, crunchy packet of

CREATIVE PLAY AND THE ARTS 49

pasta in time to music while I washed up. I knew it couldn't last and that one day they would start to notice the toys other children played with. I also had to consider the balance between 'fitting in' and giving them what they really needed, without compromising my values.

It was my son who presented me with one of my greatest challenges. Not long after joining pre-school, he announced that he wanted an Action Man as the other boys had them. I was horrified. I didn't think I'd be pestered until he was at least school age – an Action Man?! I made no promises but that evening I thought a lot about Action Man. I had owned one as a child, bought for me by the wondrous Aunty Peg, who always seemed to know what was needed. Robin, as my Action Man was called, was one of my most treasured toys. I don't remember him ever owning weapons; if he did I'm sure I never played with them. Robin was never rough or nasty. He had a friendly face, a fluffy jacket like my favourite teacher and enjoyed swimming in the sink with my other dolls. I wondered if a 21st century Robin could possibly exist.

Visiting the local shops I was horrified to discover that my lovely, innocent Robin had been replaced by mean-faced, thuggish dolls. Some even had guns welded to their hands so that they couldn't be removed. Inside, I wept for the children who would receive them. But my quest for Robin was not over. If he was 'old hat' then perhaps he could be found in a charity shop.

After discarding a few horrors, I soon found two cheery chaps and a scuba diver. All they needed now was clothing and it wasn't going to be military! Before long, the dolls were transformed into a 'rainbow warrior', a fisherman with sweater and beanie and, well, a scuba diver. My son was delighted. The dolls were instantly thrown aboard his pirate ship and set sail for adventures driven entirely by his own imagination.

My story could end there, but a year later, my mother-in-law announced that she had found a bag of my husband's old Action Men for me. Too late, the children had spotted it and were already ransacking the contents. To my delight, there were no 'nasty bits' but a bag of dolls in beautiful hand-made outfits. My husband's grandmother, it turned out, had spent long evenings lovingly transforming old clothes into costumes, including a fantastic Sotsman and a delicate leather coat made from an old glove. There were also extras such as a little tent and a pet dog. They played for hours! No one complained at the lack of weapons, or that the dolls were old. My battle with Action Man had given me a lot to think about.

It occurred to me, that toys that make their way down the generations, help children to connect with their family history; their dad took great delight at joining in with the Action Man games! The specialness of the hand-made garments also enchanted the children in a way that would be impossible with manufactured toys. It had also connected me to a woman who had died almost ten years before I met my husband, but who had been so important in his life. Freed from their original trappings, these home-finished dolls have become open-ended toys, allowing the children to play their own games. And so my son's desire for an Action Man was satisfied, I found my Robin, and I am currently pester-free. For now!

As Grandma, I love to take my grandson to the museums where there are always creative and hands-on activities for children. We have just been to the Horniman Museum where he took part in 'What Mr Horniman Forgot to Collect' and 'Top Hat and Tales with Mr Horniman'. He loved it and it was all free!

Yesterday I went to a halloween party where the whole class was invited. It is rare for parties to happen in the child's own house. The party bags were filled with plastic 'nasties'. One private party where there were only eight children there was a wonderful treasure hunt. Individuals found treasures which ended up as their

CREATIVE PLAY AND THE ARTS 51

party bags – a present which they had earned.

What you need to do is to feed your children's enthusiasms.

If children are in the house all the time their play is hampered. Parents are very fearful however. I go to the 'One-O-Clock Club' on the heath – a hut with painting and play dough. Outside with bikes and slide and physical activities, mothers meet and chat. Play is no longer ever unsupervised in the way it was for my daughter as a child BUT unstructured play outside with adults at a distance is possible.

Children have less and less opportunity to be independent as parents become more and more fearful of unsupervised play. This limits children's individual development and responsibility for their own decisions that is invaluable in producing children who can think for themselves.

When watching television, my son becomes the characters on screen; he acts them out with great intensity. Mostly this is positive but with some programmes it is all too much e.g. 'Tarzan' and 'The Incredibles'. He then becomes over-the-top and rather hyper and aggressive. It is not a good experience.

I have to limit the TV and get them out in the garden; it's pushing them in that direction and showing them that there are other things to do.

My daughter aged three and I (her dad) were playing in the sun in the garden. The washing had dried and I had taken the double white sheet and floated it over her as she lay on a rug. This wonderful sense of being slowly enclosed as the cotton white covered the sky and sank softly down all around I remembered myself. She adored it. "Again!" she shrieked. And again and again till I said "Enough! Let's fold it up and go down to the stream".

She took a corner like I did; then found the other like I did; and then brought them together and held them tight. Then the little miracle occurred. Without me saying a word, she let go with one hand and found the new corner she had made with the other. I followed suit. We did it again and, then, clasping her corners of this new and neat long rectangle, she walked towards me and joined them with mine. She then carried the one pound square of cotton indoors.

When her mum returned, I was shouting with laughter as I held them both at this huge achievement of our beautiful daughter.

One hot summer's day, my daughter aged eight and three friends in bathing suits splashed their way down the stream from the dipping pool to the pond beyond the lane. The dipping pool has been formed by the winter floods cascading over a trunk and gouging out stones to waist-high. The stream then winds on for half a mile, under branches and past bushes and over stones and is quickly out of sight of the house. The stones are slippery, the water is chilly, the branches can snap back so you have to take care of each other. If you play by the rule of always having one foot in the water, the pond beyond the lane can only be reached by crawling through the tunnel. And where the water pours into the pond, it is deep enough to cover your head and wide enough to have to swim to shore. There was the pure delight of giggling camaraderie formed in a thrilling adventure, ungoverned or suggested by adults. A new view of the world: she can now envisage being a stone, a branch, a fish, a bird or a dragonfly!

I have a photograph of my daughter aged four with her finger apparently gripped tight by the sharp beak of a huge stone eagle in the gardens of a large country house. She is acting the pain perfectly.

We have fun in playing as a family; an informal kick-about, ball games in the park, a sing-song, painting a mural…..

There is a problem with sibling rivalry and one trying to catch up with the other – endlessly comparing, unfavourably. Time with two children – giving them both individual time alone with my undivided attention – can help.

Our children love trips on the Docklands Light Railway in London. It is driver-less, computer operated so that they can pretend to be the drivers if they can get in the front seats. On a fine day we take a picnic to stop off at the Royal Observatory Grand Park or visit the Cutty Sark. As they are both under eleven it is free for them and each accompanied by an adult.

There is a wonderful café in Kensal Rise opened by mums. Lovely food and fantastic play area for kids. Attached is an alternative medicine, reflexology, aromatherapy clinic.

Provide the opportunities to join activities like Brownies, horse-riding, amateur drama group; everything that helps the child use all their creativity and imagination, nurturing their self-expression, self-control, discipline and confidence outside the home and honing their social skills.

Involve the child in the handling of dangerous objects. At three, a child can light a match and carry a candle – with supervision. They will learn how dangerous and precarious this element can be but gain confidence rather than fear. Teach them to use a sharpish knife – cut up vegetables or shave down a pencil or fashion a piece of wood. Light a fire in the garden and brew up some tea or a pan of milk for hot chocolate.

Very young children do not demand complex toys to play with, or rather to work with. Simple kitchen utensils are satisfying to work with bringing out their initiative and creativity. As soon as they are given complex gadgets which do more or all of the work for them, they tend to go along with them, making for more passivity and less initiative. They are very much guided by the adults who might aim at bigger and 'better' toys to please them or sometimes to make up for the lack of opportunity to be with them more.

Their taste for simple tools to work with coincides with the strong desire to imitate the adults and a wooden cooking spoon and sieve can give endless pleasure. Similarly when they are old enough a real trowel and fork are preferable to elaborate gardening sets. This does not mean that miniature toys are not as welcome; whether sets for dolls or farm models.

Children grow so quickly and it is easy to forget the memorable moments. I have made a 'memory box'. I have an envelope handy and when we have done something we want to remember, we put a souvenir in it. Every year – a new envelope – all put in a box at the back of the wardrobe – for viewing and remembering in the faraway future.

If you have a patio or paving stones in your garden try sending your children out with a box of coloured chalks and ask them if they would like to make pictures on the slabs. They usually like the idea of something which seems vaguely 'not allowed' and it is easily hosed down later.

Creativity – not as a means to an end; producing something and labelling it – rather a moment by moment experience of living; of creating one's own life as one expresses oneself in different ways; not for exhibition, exam marks, competition. Life is not an exam. It is a living developmental experience, flowing naturally with growth.   Music is an essential part of this non-verbal expression and communication. The senses of touch and smell tend to be neglected with too much emphasis on the visual. Foster an understanding of the value of exchange – that is not always for money.

A very little girl sat in the back of Grandpa's car holding one finger of her Nana's hand. They smiled at each other all the way down the bumpy track, with many and many a "Hello Becki".... "Awwo Nana"... being exchanged. When we finally got to the stream running past the church, out we rushed, ready to play a completely new game – 'Pooh Sticks'. This adorable very little person shrieked with delight as the sticks emerged from under the huge stone slab of a bridge......All this was ten years ago now and the photo of us both by the side of the stream – she in red tartan kilt and me with tartan scarf to match – brings the softest smile of love to my face, every time I look at it.

Chapter 6
Keeping in Touch With Nature

Children's voices in the orchard
Between the blossom and the fruit-time.
'Landscapes' by T. S. Eliot

Human beings are part of the natural world: we follow the rhythm of its seasons with celebrations. The sheer wonder of its creation is in all of us but is clearest in the very young and we need to nourish and sustain that affinity as they grow.

In the past, children in rural areas enjoyed the run of the fields and the woods; after the Second World War, an increasing number of families in the towns were much more restricted (although they could explore the bomb sites redolent with pink rosebay willow herb). Now families are moving back to villages where a school is still functioning and one of the reasons is to bring up their children in close contact with nature, even though much of farm land is now out of bounds and footpaths are being closed.

The obstacles to free contact with the natural world have already been mentioned: traffic, fear of molestation and enclosures. But there is still plenty of opportunity for children to enjoy the natural world, although parents have to take a supervisory role to get to parks and the countryside and then their presence can be protection at a distance and participating only when invited.

If acclimatised from the very beginning to all varieties of weather, children will accept rain, wind, snow and sunshine in their stride which is just as well, because they are likely to face greater extremities by the time they grow up. Nurseries and schools are now springing up that make the great outdoors their classrooms and they are enjoying considerable popularity. Most of us are tied to formal schools, however, but these can be greatly enhanced by raised gardens in the playground, which can make school dinners attractive with cultivation of vegetables and fruit. This also goes for those who are lucky enough to have a garden or a family allotment, now in demand with long waiting lists. Fruit trees, however, can be grown in containers and vegetables in grow-bags, not forgetting pot plants, and most urban children can have some experience of growing their own. Nest boxes are possible in limited space and further afield in the country, there are plans to provide for the protection of various species of wild life that have been deprived of their natural habitat.

It is also a joy when children can care for a pet, paving the way for the caring that is expected in adult life. They could start with small species such as hamsters and gerbils and progress as they grow older. However calls on their time do increase with age, so there is always the matter of what sort of pet can realistically be coped with. A dog is often the ultimate pet and could be a family responsibility; a tall order, bearing in mind that dogs generally need a free run twice a day. Of course if the conditions are favourable and the family co-operate, it is an excellent way of getting enough exercise in all weathers.

In nurturing children's love of the whole of the natural world we are paving the way for the next generation to be active in doing what they can to preserve the planet. This should be an integral part of their lives, closely related to their appreciation of what nature offers as a positive approach, rather than dwelling on the disasters that might be in store. So we give ecological explanations of why we choose to walk or take public transport, for example, not forgetting the added bonus of exercise in the fresh air and contact with the natural world. Similarly, we state the environmental case with regard to growing our own organic food and show the proof of the pudding, which children will appreciate. In school the care of the planet should permeate all areas of the curriculum and not be relegated to a particular slot. If we take action on a cause to protect the environment, our children will register this and even join in where appropriate. Of course, in our approach we need to be aware of their particular stage of development, but it is generally agreed that young people are often more conscious of the need to do one's bit in conserving the planet than many adults.

A hundred parents of children with attention-deficit-disorder found that they reacted better after playing in 'green spaces'. They concluded that time spent in a natural setting fostered more creative play, required greater interaction between children and ultimately boosted their communication and thinking skills.

It is encouraging to know that, according to the recent UNICEF Report (2007) already referred to, in schools that had actively engaged children and addressed their worries about the environment by providing environmental projects as part of their education, the children were happier. The sense that "we can do something" made all the difference.

Parents' contributions

"If the educator and the student lose their relationship to nature, to the trees, to the rolling sea, they will certainly lose their relationship with man". J Krishnamurti

My daughter had a wonderful day learning survival techniques with Ray Mears as a prize in a national competition linked to Ordinance Survey's Free Maps for 11 year olds. She learnt how to track, mimic the deer's mating call, lighting a fire using only raw materials, dowsing it and leaving the place as they found it without a trace of their exploits.

My two boys are attending a nursery that stays outdoors in all weathers. They are well-wrapped up and their days are devoted to nature walks, rearing chickens, 'mud play', climbing trees and vegetable gardening. Their playground is the forest with a shelter they have made out of wattle and daub. When it gets cold they light a bonfire and play running around games.

We try to get out in the fresh air as often as we can as a family. Here are some of the outings we have had: a visit to a farm with a picnic: a kite-flying session with home-made kites: organised a treasure hunt in our local park. We often join with other families or take turns.

Time spent in nature is the first experience necessary for children's healthy growth and learning. The child may wish sometimes to be solitary. We need to find ways in which we can safely give that time to our children – to be close by but to give them the opportunity to be on their own and to go within themselves. Time spent on their own is as important as time spent with other children in nature because the 'inner life' can then develop. Children find peace through playing together in nature too.

They have started asking me the names of trees and flowers when we go into the park and so we take little books:*Flowers for the Children* and *Trees for the Children* when we go.

There are so many plants that can be grown in containers if you haven't a garden: fruit trees, salad and vegetables and every sort of flower.

Keeping in touch with Nature is as necessary as breathing...to provide the child with access to nature, be it a garden, woods or park is invaluable. Here they have the freedom from cars and have tranquility. They learn about trees, flowers and creatures. They learn respect for the environment. They can learn to love such places thus always providing a haven for mind, spirit and body throughout their entire lives.

My children love growing their own vegetables in their plots and then harvesting and cooking them. We make home-made remedies and skin products. A simple one for children is to grow pot marigold (calendula) and harvest the petals and put them into a nice oil base and leave in the sun for the summer. This calendula will protect faces in the cold, dry weather or can be used for any sore places. The child begins to understand how useful nature is if we work with it in these ways. We also pick lime blossom and dry it, using it for a calming tisane. Like everything else, when they learn these things young, it sticks. We always like to stay in tune with the changing seasons and I notice my daughter now also notices, so we pick and cook blackberries in the late summer.
Talk about the sun, moon, and stars sometimes. "Let's look at the moon tonight and imagine we are standing on a large football."

Keep the child in touch with the seasons. Name the trees and plants that surround you. Welcome the diversity of season and weather. When it rains let them wallow in wetness and splash in puddles. Take them on wild, windy walks; into woods one week and up hills the next. Let them have leaf fights before giving them the job of sweeping up and burning them (the leaves), or composting them.

Almost all children want a pet and this can be impossible but wild birds are easily encouraged. (The robin adopts families and gardens the whole year round and is incredibly tame once a pattern is established.)

At the end of the road where we lived was a farm and we three and our friends had the freedom to play in the fields and a small copse, picking daisies, buttercups and bluebells to take home. Especially on May Day we would collect a basket of delicate mauve lesser-stitchwort, known to us as may-flowers, dress-up and take them around to our mothers. Our parents would take us for long walks in the countryside and on holiday in the Lake District. Then we would always have a book with us to identify the wild flowers and thus gained appreciation for the beauty of nature.

Create Nature Memories. A vivid memory for me and my daughter – it was autumn – November. Walking in the sunlit park with a friend and my four year-old daughter, we kicked up the newly-fallen crimson, yellow flaming leaves and threw them up in the air before trying to bury her. The leaves whirled, we whirled and all was laughter. We then returned home in the fading light.

We go 'leafing' especially in the autumn when they are so lovely. We take them home and find out their names and label them which is a good introduction to reading.

We try to have an outdoor family expedition once a month, according to the seasons, such as summer star-gazing, autumn fungal foray.

We have emphasis on healthy fun and exercise – as the old saying goes; 'the family that plays together stays together and stays healthy and happy'.

Childhood is a time of discovering the world through creative play. When they are young they seem to have a sense of affinity towards the wondrous world of nature and we can help sustain and nourish this propensity.

Instead of party bags we gave out a packet of sunflower seeds and a plastic pot. This puts children in touch with nature while rejecting consumer society and giving pleasure in creativity.

I have a photograph of my daughter aged six peeking over the noses of her Aunt's two horses nuzzling each other. Everybody likes each other.

One thing I may do when I can is what many others are doing, or thinking of doing – leaving London. Where I live there is almost no green space for children, not even a swimming pool for five miles!

We are blessed to live amidst beautiful countryside and are looking to involve the children in outdoor pursuits, with a view to developing active healthy pastimes. We have built camps in our woods, picnicked outdoors, and held a 'cowboy camp' for friends' families. The children went 'mountaineering' today on the fells with their own little maps and chocolate coins to find in a secret location – they were thrilled to find a little bit of snow on the ridge, to be the one to first spot the footpath sign etc. Our son painted a picture of a stone in the field where they had been playing with the moss, and used a few colours because he had observed it.

They had a horse-riding lesson as a treat on dad's birthday – our daughter particularly enjoyed it and is saving up her pocket money for another lesson. We explained that it does cost quite a lot but if she saved half then we will match fund it and that if she wants to, she can earn extra pocket-money by helping or put birthday money towards it.

We have a vegetable garden planned but await a local farmer bringing us some topsoil; then we will have a go and watch our seeds germinate and develop. I think it is good for children to see 'slow miracles' in a speeded-up world. And of course, we hope to eat some of our crops and furnish the rabbits.

The pets are an attempt to get the children to focus on something real and interactive. We hope to get hens soon and a dog, once William is walking. This will force us all out into the fresh air and help us make use of our field and little woodland. It probably all sounds a bit idyllic – it is sometimes more than others. Like all parents we get some bits 'right' and some bits not; we have concerns for our children but we are doing the best we can to equip them to love life and love learning and live life to the full.

Children have a great sense of wonder. We take them for a walk in the moonlight and go at their pace. They discover all sorts of creatures with a torch. Our daughter said "Oh look at the moon's gone to sleep with that tree!" We try to let them lead and discover the world.

I have just heard that children from Normandy in France are being taken to school in horse-drawn vehicles. This certainly brings them into contact with nature, saves petrol, produces manure and is so good for the environment.

"I want the stars in my eyes to last forever!" my four year old.

"The children were playing about, but they never looked at the lovely spring day. They had no need to look, for they were spring, their laughter and their play were part of the tree, the leaf, and the flower. You felt this, you didn't imagine it. It was as though the leaves and the flowers were taking part in the laughter, in the shouting, and in the balloon that went by. Every blade of grass, the yellow dandelion, and the children were part of the whole earth. The dividing line between Man and Nature disappeared."
J. Krishnamurti (from *The Only Revolution*)

"Man did not weave the web of life – he is merely a strand in it. Whatever he does to the web, he does to himself." Chief Seattle.

"As humans we are born of the Earth, nourished by the Earth, healed by the earth." Thomas Berry

Chapter 7
Care of the Body: Exercise, Sleep and Food

"Happiness is beneficial for the body."
Marcel Proust

Exercise

"Success depends in a very large measure upon individual initiative and exertion."
Anna Pavlova

The child's body knows what it needs – plenty of exercise of all descriptions: running, jumping, hopping, skipping, so that all parts of the body are brought into action. The traditional games, handed down from one generation to the next, helped to satisfy this need, together with all the other games that children invent.

Right from babyhood it is the nature of children to be constantly on the move. There are various stories of adults imitating three to four year-olds in everything they do and they only managed to keep going for three minutes, and that in a state of complete exhaustion! We can observe children unfolding physically, each activity programmed naturally to prepare for the next stage: sitting up, crawling, toddling, walking, running, then the world is their oyster or should be if possible. Their basic need for fresh air and outdoor play has always been essential for well-being, both physical and mental.

Let us concentrate on the sheer delight that young children

have in physical play and games and hope that a solution can be found within the various possibilities of recreation open to modern children so that their physical health is not impaired.

Lack of physical exercise is emphasized in the chapters on 'Creative Play and the Arts', 'Keeping in Touch with Nature' and 'Keeping Technology in Control' and this points to the risk of creating a generation of 'couch potatoes' – and 'slouch potatoes' with regard to posture. If too much time is spent bending over a computer, the whole body's posture can suffer, leading to muscular tension and back pain. Spending hours huddled over desks or tables that are too low and on chairs that do not support the back is a recipe for later trouble.

Regular exercise and taking of breaks can counter the worst effects of this sedentary life, but there has to be a new look at furniture design for both pupils in schools and adults in offices.

Millions of British school children risk back injury by struggling to school with over-laden bags: the average child lugs two pounds to school every day. Backpacks worn on both shoulders should be the order of the day, even if they are seen as 'uncool' by the child's peers (but not on one shoulder, which is the most harmful way of bearing any weight). The charity Back Care campaigns for adequate school-locker space as well as for orthopaedically designed school furniture and this would help greatly towards solving this problem.

Research shows that six out of ten pupils complain of back pain at some point and much of this can be blamed on the low tables and stackable plastic bucket chairs now common in schools. Back Care is launching a campaign for these to be replaced with adjustable forward-tilting chairs and angled desks that hark back to the Victorian era. British ergonomic designers of furniture say that educationists now realise that good posture can improve concentration, performance and behaviour but, of course, it costs more money in the short-term.

Parents' contributions

I read that researchers have found that three year-old Scottish children weigh more than their counterpart of twenty-five years ago – owing to lack of exercise; and this pattern was maintained when they were five years old. A decline in children's physical abilities since the 1960s has also been recorded in Japan.

As a parent you grow with your child and it takes hard work and perseverance. You can enjoy all sorts of exercise with them but "don't call it exercise – call it an adventure!"

Your body is like a machine – what you put in you will get out. It gives you energy and gets you in a good mood.

The great outdoors is so much more delightful for children and adults alike. It is magical, allows spontaneity and is free!

My parents really understood the need for children to be out of doors. I have an early memory of being under an improvised canopy attached to the kitchen wall, on a rug playing with buttons while my baby sister slept nearby. The older we got, the further we wandered; at first down our lengthy garden, then the alleyway behind (watched over, no doubt, by the entire neighbourhood!), then with friends on the street and finally chasing the poor milkman for miles on our bikes. I was fortunate enough to be brought up in a very traditional family. Gran lived in an old cottage about ten minutes' walk from our house. My parents looked after her and she looked after my sister and I; or rather, she walked the legs off us! She walked us to Chapel, she took us firewood hunting, taught us which berries we could eat and even took us to an old clay pit where we made models for hours on end. No one ever complained about the mess. We managed all this despite living on the outskirts of a large city, in a very working-class district. We somehow found green space that could pass as countryside. When my own children were born, I wanted to give them the same rich childhood, whatever my circumstances.

My daughter was born while we were living in a fourth floor flat, so I just opened the balcony door and let the sunshine in! We rolled on the mat and later, she bounced in her chair. I had no car, so I chose the prettiest routes when out walking. We finally bought a house and soon our ten-month-old was crawling barefoot through the spring sunshine warmed grass, feeling the great outdoors between her toes for the first time. It was a lovely day. We dug the vegetable patch, Kate (well-wrapped except toes) crawled around in delight and even the cat joined in. My children's love of the great outdoors has continued to grow as I have seized every opportunity to get out and have fun. It has given the children healthy bodies and souls and given me a magical set of memories, including dancing in a huge puddle by our back door in the rain with a two-year-old!

Care of the body denotes respect for the entire person. Nurturing it with sleep, good nourishing food and giving it the exercise it desires i.e. swimming, walking and sports. Enough sleep enables a child to concentrate at school.

I think that there is too much fear about not letting young children out of the house and this can amount to paranoia, stirred up by the media on the dangers from strangers, who might be paedophiles and murderers.

Several of us parents had a rota to walk the children during October 'Walk to School Month'. We are trying to continue in spite of objections from the children.

Sleep

"To sleep...perchance to dream."
William Shakespeare

One cannot overestimate the enormous importance of enough restful sleep, although individuals vary considerably. Over twenty-four hours it is estimated that infants between three and eleven months need fourteen to fifteen hours sleep; toddlers between twelve and thirty-six months need twelve to fourteen hours; preschoolers between three to six years need ten to eleven hours; and those of junior school age, from seven to eleven years, need ten to eleven hours. According to research, today's children in general are having at least one and often two hours fewer sleep than they need, and babies often have two or even three hours fewer. (*Toxic Childhood*, Sue Palmer)

The younger they are the greater the need for adequate sleep, particularly during the first year of life. This is because the brain processes all of the information gained during the day and stores it. As the brain is at its most active during sleep, it is essential that there is enough sleep to deal with it.

It is not difficult to pinpoint the causes of this general lack of sleep on the part of most children. The biggest sinner is without doubt the presence of a television in the bedroom. It is estimated that over 80 per cent of young children have a TV in their bedroom and that percentage is increasing. Besides being deprived of adequate sleep, the stimulating and often frightening programmes and flashing images create an unquiet atmosphere, far from the tranquility and peace needed. There should be no electronic devices in the bedroom, including mobile phones and computers, until at least teenage years and ideally not even then. Parents need to convince their children that they must have adequate restful sleep in order to function during the day.

Parents' contributions

We started early with our first born – to bed at 6.30 p.m. in a quiet, dimmed room with no distractions and it worked. The second one was more restless but eventually settled down. I felt awful when I did not rush to lift him when he woke in the middle of the night, but sometimes he did settle down of his own accord. We decided not to start lullabies or stories at bedtime too early, to let them get into the habit of going to sleep on their own. Now they are older the bedtime story is a regular routine, often with made-up stories.

It is not surprising that a newly-born baby requires so much sleep – such is the learning curve, perhaps never so great again in their whole lives. And the rate of growth is stupendous!

Our two children are so different: one wanted quite a long nap in the afternoons until she was three, the other could hardly bring himself to put his head down.

The importance of a healthy diet

"Let food be your medicine and medicine be your food."
Hippocrates

Latest figures suggest that by 2050, 60 per cent of men, half of all women and one in four children will be obese. Campaigners say it's a public health crisis which demands radical thinking about the food we eat, the exercise we do, even the way our homes and towns are designed. Statistics from the most recent large-scale survey in the UK reveal that 25 per cent of boys and 33 per cent of girls aged between two and nineteen years are overweight or obese – and there's little sign that the incidence is reducing. Quite simply, many children do little exercise and eat a diet that's packed with junk food. The problems start early in life. A survey by *Mother & Baby* magazine in 2004 revealed that nine out of ten toddlers eat junk food, with chocolate, biscuits, crisps, fish fingers, chips, cake and chicken nuggets appearing in their top ten favourite foods.

Children whose mothers work full-time while they are in the first few years of primary school are more likely to be obese when they reach sixteen than those whose mothers stay home, a US study concluded. The findings do not show why maternal employment has such an effect in mid-childhood, but suggest the link could be that this period is when food preferences and habits become established.

We cannot separate the need for exercise of the body from the equal importance of a good healthy diet. There is plenty of advice on what constitutes healthy eating, for example, five different portions of fresh fruit and vegetables per day, and a balance of protein, fats (omega 3 and 6, avoiding hydrogenated fats) and carbohydrate. The importance of DHA fat is stressed over and over again (although this has recently been challenged).

Up to a quarter of pupils have some form of learning disorder and when under-achieving children with motor difficulties were given fish oil supplements they made stunning improvements in reading and spelling and most benefits were seen in an improved attention-span and better behaviour from pupils with ADHD. In a survey of 117 under-achieving primary school age children with motor difficulties, those who were given fish oil supplements made great gains in reading and spelling. There is cause to suspect that up to a quarter of the school-age population have some sort of learning impediment caused by lack of the omega 3 fatty acids found in oily fish and green vegetables (Alex Richardson, Oxford University, published in the *TES* Scotland, March 2006).

DHA helps the brain make connections and enhances its function. It is found in some infant formulas, dietary supplements and fish, and breastfeeding is also a very important source of this fat. A Japanese research team found that a deficiency in fatty acids (omega 3 and omega 6) is having a negative effect on children's behaviour.

Jamie Oliver has been a pioneer in raising a clarion call for healthy school dinners and recently for nourishing packed lunches and we parents need to continue his campaign in our homes. Apparently the numbers of pupils taking school dinners has declined since the meals have become healthier, so it is a question of initiating good eating habits in the home. Like everything else, food habits start early in life and they are notorious for causing friction between parent and child. It is therefore especially important to start as you want to go on and this is easier with the first-born child. For example, give milk or water rather than even watered-down fruit juice and no fizzy drinks as they can contain caffeine as well as large amounts of sugar. The best way to introduce new food is to give a tiny portion and if they don't like it, make no fuss; you can try again later. In any case, small portions can be more attractive with the option of seconds. Avoid making the meal table a battleground.

We all know the attraction that junk food has for the young, and not so young, and it need not be banned from the diet altogether but it should not be regarded as a treat. In any case, it has to be an exception to the daily menu. There is also a limited place for convenience foods like whole meal takeaways or fish and chips. Convenience food can relieve the busy parent who has to cook but one should measure this against the cost, lack of freshness and possible additives. Not everyone can cultivate their own vegetables and fruit, but if it is at all possible it is worth it – taste-wise, health-wise and pocket-wise – and increasingly available organic foods can be worth the extra cost if home-grown is not feasible.

There are often different names for manufactured food but the one thing they have in common is uncertainty about what they contain. True, there are now more rules about labelling so that to some extent less salt, sugar and fat are indicated, but is not easy to assess the quality of the meat and fish used. It should be absolutely fresh when prepared, cooked in fresh oil, etc. and frozen or chilled immediately, but it is hard to be sure. If you cook it yourself, you are certain of the ingredients.

There is growing publicity on the whole issue of convenience food, especially on television, and recent reports show clearly the dangers, such as certain additives which have been shown to cause hyperactivity in children. Firms are vocal in defending the qualities of their products, saying that they are a gift to busy adults, saving them time shopping, preparing and cooking. Of course, this is a valid point and it would be tilting at windmills to oppose all use of convenience foods. Another aspect to be aware of is the danger of becoming addicted, especially to food that contains too much sugar, fat and salt. Children are particularly vulnerable; it is easy for them to become addicted to chips and turkey twizzlers for example, at a very early age. As conflict between parents and offspring is often caused by food choices and refusal by the child is a weapon for them to use in rebellion, the situation for parents is becoming much more challenging.

Although it is time-consuming to cook and much more so to encourage and help children to produce their own efforts, it is well worth it, be it stuffed dates with almonds or later on, pasta with tomato sauce. There are at least three major benefits: children get pleasure from their own creativity and the self-confidence that this engenders; they are much more likely to eat their own creations, even with relish; and it strengthens the bond with their parents.

Parents' contributions

My two-year-old already associates highly publicised, branded food with 'fun' when it is viewed in the form of cartoons and well-known characters from TV.

When my kids have commercially produced carbonated soft drinks, I worry about their teeth. Though my concern is based on sugar levels, there are a host of other ingredients on the label with doubtful-sounding names.

Meals are taken much of the time at a table with the TV off and everybody present so that there is conversation between all family members. This seems to help with learning, understanding of the world we live in and social development. It seems to help too with self-esteem since the children's knowledge, viewpoint and sense of responsibility are valued. The food, it goes without saying, is as healthy as possible, though again, the children are not altogether denied what the average child regards as particularly nice, even if not good for the body.

My advice to new parents would be "Don't compromise!" There is always another way to encourage them to eat healthy food, especially if we start as we mean to go on; very small portions of new food and no fuss if they don't like it. Try again later!

We are not easily led parents and we do not feed our children junk. In fact, our children's diet and education are paramount. We are selective of what they watch and firm with routine, boundaries and bedtime. I believe this makes our children secure and happy. You must take the lead.

It is much cheaper to breastfeed besides being the right food for human babies, just as cow's milk is absolutely right for calves.

Our two children have quite different patterns of eating: Joan will eat everything up, George eats for energy and then wants to go off to play and we have to insist that he stays at the table. Sometimes he just won't eat anything and we have to be very strict and make him eat his lunch at supper-time with nothing in between and unless he is unwell he usually does.

If the children ever say, "I don't like mushrooms … or tomato sauce," they have to try it and then we start again another day. They always have to try. They change like the wind, so we never know what they will not like next time. Therefore it is always; "They will like it another time". They have very few sweets: only when it's Christmas or Easter or someone's birthday. They have hardly ever drunk fizzy; Savia loves it and Rowan loves it also but he has weak dentine in his teeth so mustn't drink too much.

We eat together as a family as often as we can and once a fortnight on a weekend, the children, boy eight and girl ten, choose and cook the midday meals (with a little help). They always eat it all up.

I know my daughter aged three will not starve to death if she misses a meal. I give tiny portions of healthy food when she is all set to be choosy.

If he sees I'm worried about getting an amount of healthy food down him, he'll play up (aged two and a half) to get attention, so I'm quite matter of fact.

I work in a small Montessori Nursery School. A large part of the young children's activities in the Montessori curriculum are involved with the development of practical life skills. These activities and exercises are specifically designed to enable the child to overcome the challenges he meets in his everyday life.

My colleague (whom I work with on Mondays) and I decided to begin cooking with the children on a Monday and ever since we have all helped to prepare 'The Monday Lunch'. Between eight and ten children from age three and a half to six come into the kitchen on Monday mornings. In the beginning we had no specific expectations other than occupying the children with meaningful tasks to help them develop practical life skills. For the first couple of weeks the menu was dinosaur-themed, so we had 'Dino Hatchlings' which were just hot dogs with pepper eyes and tongue coming out of a baked potato, mayo., ketchup and egg. And the next week we made 'Dino Swamp Soup'. After that we started doing appley recipes to coincide with Apple Fortnight. We got the children making apple and celery soup, apple and sausage rolls, apple puffs, apple pudding, etc. So, apart from those initial two weeks we have not used anything gimmicky or 'child friendly' to entice the children (like ketchup for example). We have not needed to because quite unexpectedly and quite remarkably a transition in the children was taking shape. To understand this better on paper I need to first explain what stage these children were at when we started. Two of them had peeled before and chopped, the rest were absolute beginners. Apart from a couple of children, none of them were noted for their staying power (if you know what I mean!) Only about three of them could stick with a task for any length of time and the rest all had their (convincing at times) reasons, for being unwilling to, examples being defeatism to the point of giving up before event starting, timidity, lack of confidence, silliness, defiantly refusing to co-operate, and one who was convinced she would hurt herself if she did anything.

Although all the children had some experience of cookery, few had worked from raw ingredients to a finished meal on a plate. We believe that is one criteria for the transformation from unwillingness (for all the above reasons) to happy, hard-working children.

We have witnessed another transformation in the children's tastes and food tolerances. My previous healthy food experience with the children had been discouraging to say the least; 85 per cent of the children who took part in a healthy lunch with interesting and tasty foods for them to try out, would not even think about trying a food they had never eaten before. Their normal routine is a packed lunch from home which tends to be very unsurprising (and unappetizing in my opinion!) in its content. So when we embarked on this cookery project and began on unusual and unknown tastes and textures of food for the children to prepare and eat, we just did it without thinking about it too much and kept our fingers crossed. We didn't even dream that all the children would not only try everything and sit and eat their lunches; they actually enjoyed it and asked for more. This has continued for the last thirteen weeks.

Participating in cooking together develops in the child's self-esteem, a feeling of worthiness that they share.

"Children become not only users of the world but producers" Montanaro, *Understanding the Human Being*.

The children improve their motor capacities with the satisfaction and reward of a tangible and edible result. This in turn improves their self-confidence. They are both learning practical life skills to allow them more independence and they are learning what it means to cooperate and pull together as a team.

They learn about good housekeeping practices, social skills, table manners and healthy eating habits. They begin to identify different ingredients and where they come from, what they taste like and how they can complement each other. Another very important fact they learn is that meals need to be prepared and that it takes time and some effort, but that effort doesn't hurt especially when you're in a group that has fun too. We add funny songs and very corny jokes into the mix every Monday to keep the day chugging along. A favourite joke is still "How are you peeling today?"

The children are all involved in clearing, cleaning and washing up after our lovely meals together. They know now that this is all part of the job and they mostly get on with it.

The practical life skills that the children learn through cooking on a Monday are numerous. Her are some of the main ones: peeling, grating, chopping, mixing, sieving, juicing, whisking, washing fruit and veg, food combining, using a mixer and food processor, separating eggs, rolling pastry, weighing, making moulds and shaping dough, pouring, ladling, laying the table, clearing up, washing up, drying up, putting things away, opening tins, seasoning, spreading, using kitchen utensils and one four-plus year-old learnt what a knife and fork are for, having only ever used her fingers up to the point that we asked her not to, and she then resorted to lowering her mouth on to the food on her plate!!

We have had lots of positive feedback from parents about how their children are interested in what's happening in the kitchen and want to join in and help. Some children have gone home with the cookery files that we have compiled for them and made their Monday meals again at home with their families.

We have been encouraged by parents' feedback on their children's new eating habits and food tolerances. A few parents told us their sons would have never touched soup before 'Gourmet Mondays' began and now they love it. One child, however, won't accept the word soup, preferring to call it 'Dinosaur Swamp'. "I forgot to ask if the Swamp still needs the celery 'trees' in it". Another child had very strong and very particular eating preferences often driving his mum to distraction in her attempt to give him a balanced diet. Many children today are opting to not try out new tastes as they've wised-up to the fact that their mums (and dads, but mostly mums), in their desperation to get their child to eat anything, will pander to them and their tastes, allowing all sorts of bland and unbalanced diets to creep in, just to keep their child 'happy' and eating.

We have seen that children happily try out, and mostly enjoy, new tastes every Monday. The reason for this must have something to do with a) the child being very involved with the meal-making from start to finish and b) the camaraderie within the group, and we believe almost an unspoken agreement that to reject or refuse to eat the meal at the end of all their hard work together would be letting all the others down.

So to transport this recipe for success into the home, parents need to see the importance of involving their child in the meal-making process right from the start, including the decision-making on what to prepare (which the children also do on Mondays). Looking through a cookery book with your child can be very rewarding, especially with all the great photographs of food. Keep a notepad close by to jot down ideas together on what to make today, tomorrow, next week etc. and, throughout the actual food preparation, be a team, even if there are only two of you. Encourage at every opportunity and let the child feel like the important member of the team. Show the children how everything is done, the whole process and keep the "only a grown up can do this" stuff to an absolute minimum. Children love to chop – give them a board and a knife and show them how to. We've found that a decent eating knife with a good blade will chop most fruit and veg. nicely and is less likely to chop a finger accidentally. Remembering that we all have accidents in the kitchen but perhaps if we'd been shown how to do things properly when we were young then we'd have less of them now?

As a student of Maria Montessori's work, I would like to conclude this piece from her point of view, which was that practical life exercises, more than any other occupation undertaken by children during the stages of development we are working with, work in developing the whole child: physically, mentally and morally. She strongly believed that it is through manual activity that the child reaches a higher level of intelligence and that whoever has worked with his hands has a stronger character, through his own organisation of his true personality.

So we must as adults make our primary duty towards the child be in assisting him to perform useful acts. (59.88 *The Discovery of the Child* by M. Montessori)

I find the children's menus tempting price-wise but too often the food is deep-fried. We try to order half-portions of the variety offered to adults.

It has been difficult to persuade doting aunts and grandparents not to give too many sweets and chocolates but we're working on it.

Now that the children are older, they are taking an interest in making sense of the ingredients listed on products, keeping an eye out for sugar and hydrogenated fats.

With all things it is best to avoid extremes. For parents of young children it is particularly important to get them used to fruit and vegetables at a very early age and then the chances of getting addicted to a limited 'children's menu' diet are greatly lessened. So many cafes and restaurants list the usual chips, turkey twizzlers, chicken pieces and ice cream and at the cheaper price it can be tempting.

It is tempting to get ready meals when time is short; the difficulty is to know about their origin, freshness and preparation. Are the chicken pieces free-range for example?

We keep to regular times for breakfast and early supper and make it as leisurely as possible so there is no going off to school clutching a piece of toast. Food habits come very early. I started my two when they were four and a half months, with varied tiny tasters and try later for those they discard. You can't start too young; fresh, healthy food right from the start. Then they don't get addicted to fizzy drinks and junk food.

Chapter 8
Happy Schooling

'The secret of education lies in respecting the pupil'.
Ralph Waldo Emerson

Education is the process of bringing out and nurturing every child's natural propensity to know about the world they live in. As we have seen, this starts from babyhood and can continue throughout life. Educators, including of course parents, have a task to respond sensitively to their children's need to explore and to learn.

So when the appropriate time comes for a child to begin nursery education, there should be a gradual continuum from their home activities: free imaginative play, songs, rhythm, dance, picture books, drawing, painting, making things and modelling. These provide a foundation on which more formal education – reading, writing, numeracy and elementary science – will be built. This approach will go with the flow of a holistic approach to learning, knowing that everything is interconnected rather than separated into little boxes.

The fact that young children do not need outside incentives to learn as they are automatically doing it both mentally and physically all the time, is a challenge to much of the present approach to formal education. Unfortunately the policy of the present government flies in the face of this challenge and is bent on young children starting the 'basics' at an ever-earlier age. So in spite of the efforts of many devoted teachers in primary schools, the emphasis is on getting down to work and not wasting too much time once compulsory schooling has begun at the age of five and often at four. This is in opposition to almost every other country in Europe, where formal schooling starts at six or even seven years old, preceded by sound preparatory work in nursery education. The children then sail through the basics in relatively little time and enjoy them as, at that stage, they can take them in their stride.

Of course, most children need guidance in learning to read and write, although it is not uncommon for children to teach themselves to read given the appropriate books, starting with picture books at an early stage. Individual children vary in their readiness to learn and this needs a very flexible approach. The great thing is not to discourage them and put them off by pushing them unduly, otherwise untold damage may be done to their whole attitude to learning and especially to their self-esteem. An atmosphere of fear and inadequacy can be created which permeates the teachers and parents as well as the children and this exacerbates the children's apprehension. There is now an increasing debate about the teaching of reading especially with regard to the teaching of phonics to pupils rather than a choice of all the options, and in the long run the criterion must be enjoyment so that reading can become a life-long habit. Before actually teaching the complex skills for reading, there needs to be continual preparation in the nursery stages in the form of picture books, story telling and being read to, learning words of interest and labelling them etc. This preparation leads naturally to the desire to read.

Having a concept of the whole before tackling the parts is also the Rudolph Steiner approach to the teaching of reading: children should understand the whole activity that they are to learn before you teach them specific skills. The need to understand what reading is for before they learn to decipher particular groups of letters.

However, it would be wrong to paint a completely negative picture of what goes on in primary schools and things have greatly improved; scrapping SATs for the very young for example. The long tradition of excellence in many British primary schools is still apparent in spite of bureaucracy, with endless form-filling and the threat of the dreaded league tables. But the pressures are there and it is hard for parents not to get swept away with them and transmit their worries to their children, who might either be stimulated to work harder or, more likely, to give up in despondency, with possible repercussions later in their secondary schooling. The pressures continue in the form of continual examinations through to GCSE and A levels and this means that the teachers feel compelled to concentrate on the examinable subjects only, often short-changing the artistic and the physical subjects as well as personal development, including citizenship.

Again I return to the recent UNICEF report which placed British children at the bottom of the league tables in terms of well-being, endorsing the need for the system of national testing itself to be examined. Seven hundred in-depth interviews with seven to eleven year olds, teachers and parents revealed a worrying level of stress and anxiety. This research questions the value of the British examination system.

In this frenzied atmosphere of competitiveness parents feel that they must give their children a head start by getting them into 'fast lane' schools, from nurseries onwards, knowing that at the secondary stage a great divide is emerging between aspiring academies and what are sometimes referred to as 'sink' schools. It would be easy to blame the parents for being pushy, but they are fully aware of the fact that they do not have the much-vaunted 'freedom of choice' of school and that the struggle for places in the transfer to secondary education can so often be a nightmare. Personal and social skills and attributes such as communication, self-esteem and self-control, are thirty-three times more important in determining earnings than academic results. Yet increasing numbers of parents are pushing their children to read books aimed at a higher age to fast track their education to the detriment of their development. Many other countries have neighbourhood schools with automatic local intake and these have been successful with a range of mixed ability pupils.

In spite of these difficulties, caused mainly by misguided government policy, a lot of good work goes on in all schools, due mostly to the dedication of the teachers. Children are marvelously adaptable and, of course, the 'high fliers' can thrive, but generally a significant number of children are not getting as fair a deal as they should and there must be change. The aim should be to make learning a pleasure and school days happy for all.

The important factor is without doubt the human contact. According to research carried out by Munich University (2004), there is no evidence that computers, elecronic white-boards, etc. make any positive difference to children's learning. Mechanical teaching does not tend to stimulate thought as questions often require only a simple tick in response. Ofsted has been instructed to castigate schools that do not make sufficient use of IT in lessons, even where there is plenty of good traditional teaching and learning in evidence. Several millions of pounds of tax payer's money are being spent by government to put computers and other technology into schools and the big tech. companies have spent much more, especially in secondary schools.

In the past there was a tendency for teachers and parents to blame each other for any problems that arose. Now there is more hope that they are able to co-operate for the well-being of their children's education, and this might be the keynote for the future. What is evident is that the overall picture is not one of happy schooling; governments, teachers and parents need to make every effort to rectify the situation. Schools need to take notice of the different approaches to learning when, according to the research of Professor Michael Sayer of Kings College, London, eleven-year-olds given cognitive tests were found on average to be two to three years behind the same age group fifteen years ago.

Parents' contributions

(Inspiration from a conference entitled 'Should Education Make you Happy?')

Over a hundred years ago a group of parents opened a school aimed at 'arousing interest in the spirit of inquiry...especially to encourage self-reliance hand-in-hand with the sympathetic faculties'. Today it has kept to these ideals manifested in an inspirational conference on the question, 'Should education make you happy – a challenge to the purpose of today's education system'.

A film made by the chair of the King Alfred School Society and the school students, entitled 'Why am I here?' showed pupils at various stages answering questions such as 'Why are you at school?' and 'Why are you alive?' The pupils responded spiritedly to these deeply philosophical questions and what came through, even with the five year-olds, was that this school was making them happy. The primary children were, however, more happily fulfilled than the older ones, who were more preoccupied with exams. The consensus on all sides was that the exam system was unfair.

All the speakers were united in criticizing the stress built up by the present educational system's excessive use of exams and league tables and they spoke in positive ways of the true potential of education and how it had been hijacked by the overwhelming demands of exams, creating a system in which pupils are groomed for work rather than given education for itself. It was an electrifying day, covering both the political and personal aspects of the question, with calls by the speakers for revolution, for children themselves to rise up, reject the current system and refuse to take exams.

Here are a few quotes from the speakers which give a sense of the whole tone of the conference.

It started with Jefferson's Declaration of Independence: "We hold these truths to be self-evident, that all men are created equal, that they are endowed by their creator with certain unalienable Rights, that among these are Life, Liberty and the pursuit of Happiness".

'We should ask ourselves what makes a human being? What is measured in exams is solely linguistic, logical aptitudes: the desire to express oneself is trampled on in the curriculum'.

'A good society is one in which there are as few miserable people as possible. Happiness can be defined as freedom and feeling in control'.

We are creating 'performance-oriented children, waiting for external validation rather than self-motivated'.

'The current system is a one-dimensional perspective on something which is multi-dimensional. Education has become managerial; bulletpoint, managerial directives are bullets indeed, shot right into the human consciousness'.

The speakers and audience were all professionals, all convinced that they had a duty to bring about a major change in the educational system for the sake of all children and young people's well-being.

To learn reading, writing and arithmetic seems important but should come at less specific ages. It seems to depend on each child and whether they are extrovert or more introvert. There should be more focusing on the whole child's development including socialising, sport and the creative arts. There are rumours that the government is now regretting the introduction of SATs exams, but unfortunately it is unlikely that they will end the one at eleven year's old.

Bullying today is partly caused by a lack of free play when children have to learn to sort out their differences without adult interference.

Happy schooling encourages a desire to learn, to achieve and to aim for excellence. It encourages cooperation amongst all sorts of people from different backgrounds. It provides a stepping-stone of cooperation in preparation for adult life. It can mean the difference between a happy confident individual or an indifferent, anti-social individual with no interest in the wonders of learning. Schooling is not only for recognised achievements but to create personal curiosity about the world we live in.

The more fancy the technology intervening between the student and subject matter/delivery system, the less human interaction and so the less the physicality of the student will be engaged. It is by forcing children to focus entirely on the mind's activities at the expense of physical engagement with the world that problems arise. A child whose physical experience of the world is limited to keyboard and pointer/mouse is being forced to negate millennia of human development. Many social scientists, anthropologists etc. acknowledge that up to 90 per cent of human communication is non-verbal or body language and honed through contact and interaction with other human beings. If this is not at the heart of any teaching system, it is not supporting a child's ability to grow in the round and to reach full potential.

I am about to embark on a new venture, and that is to become a Montessori teacher. Since becoming a parent, moving out of London and giving up my career as a make-up artist, I feel it is my duty to play an active role in my children's educational years. I believe that I cannot solely rely on the education system to ensure that my children have an enriched, balanced and happy childhood. I would like my children's teachers to nurture them in a way that suits the child and I am not sure that this is possible as class sizes are too large and I am concerned about the tests and homework at primary level. Our society today, with work and school, leaves very little family time – time for having fun. This is vital in our home. I feel that there is a rush to begin every child at four to start at the same time, rather than when the child is ready. If I had my way, I would have school start at the age of five/six and only have a four day week or part-time with good nursery schools filling the gaps if required. I do not think we take the emotional side of the children on board.

Before the intense pressure of SATs it was a time of experiential learning and I could bring in my artistic and creative talents with my pupils. My early childhood experiences with puppets inspired me to help the children create puppet plays. They made glove puppets and string ones with cotton tubes and matchboxes strung together. My student teachers brought in a large Pinocchio puppet and sometimes I took into the classroom an 18" carved marionette, dressed as a clown, which I had made at college.

The state provides education and it is easy to think that the child's development is taken care of but education encompasses much more than is provided by a school. There is a great propensity to provide additional help in the studies that children follow at school and forget that there is a whole world of additional work skills that are rarely touched upon. Think of the skills your friends may have and see if their knowledge can be incorporated into your children's lives.

'Life-skills' is a term we hear on the lips of educationalists in the context of building leadership skills and preparing students for the business world. But for a young child it can also mean how you manage to practically live your life, how to cook and grow food. These subjects are rarely taught at school nowadays but both can be seen as chemistry lessons. Physics is taught from the text book but the 21st century is brim full of new technology which is not yet addressed. This is the area where new ideas can be generated such as groundbreaking carbon-saving systems. Solar panels are in their infancy and at the moment there are not enough skilled installers to make the change easy.

Teachers have become professionally cautious due to the possibility of litigation and also because their ability to teach a rigid curriculum is constantly tested, as are the children. A climate of joyous communication which many teachers have cited as one of the reasons why they teach, is under considerable threat. It is to be celebrated that there are so many good and enjoyable schools in existence given the tight guidelines and surveillance that the government has created.

The General Teaching Council has called for exams to be scrapped for the under-sixteens because they are putting too much stress on teachers and pupils.

Will they ever learn from the well-established practice of most of the European countries that start formal schooling at the age of six or seven? This is supported by the specialists in early childhood education.

Our five year-old son became very unhappy at his primary school and after a lot of consideration, we decided to send him to a Rudolph Steiner school where he is thriving. We like the way that Steiner schools give much more time to creativity and play and that reading and writing aren't taught until the age of seven. We didn't like the way that everything was starting younger and younger at the primary school. *(See Richard House's account of Rudolph Steiner Schooling, Appendix 1.)*

There are reports from the UK, US and Japan that learning difficulties such as dyslexia are on the increase by as much as 10 per cent.

We always give books for presents to our children and as long as they are chosen according to their tastes, they can be a real, lasting pleasure. We think that this is the best contribution we can make to their education.

Home-schooling – this is a very definite way of actively influencing your children and passing on your values. We were not happy about our children being rushed into formal learning when they were obviously not ready for it, so we started home education.

Our children are all being home-educated. We continually work with other children and organisations so they do not miss out on social contact. On the contrary, it is more rewarding on an informal, mixed age group basis.

It seems my son is bullied – he finds schoolwork boring and he fidgets. Perhaps the school is too straight-laced and academic and recently he has had too many classes outside school-time. School tests show his reading age and spelling are those of a ten and a half old. He is six!

There is a lot of worry about the fact that boys are doing so much worse than girls academically. Is enough provision made for boys being two years behind in this area of their development, while being well ahead on spacial development? Should we take into consideration the part that nature plays in this? I recall that when my husband had finished playing with the electric train set he had bought for our daughters aged four and six, they wrapped the carriages in little blankets and put them to bed! Also a neighbour has a little boy who at a very early age, took his hammer to bed preferring it to a cuddly toy.

Homework. The children come back from school with 'optional' folders at five years old! There is great emphasis on 'achieving' – not allowing a child to learn at their own pace or allowing for wonderment. But as a parent, it is very easy to get caught up and competitive. To be honest, I still get caught into the school's demands but I try and supplement with more creative activities.

Our children are at a Steiner school where they oppose accelerated learning. They believe that children should never be rushed into things before they are ready.

A nine year-old girl (a friend of my daughter) started cycling to school by herself – a distance of over a mile on a fairly busy road. There was a fixed silence from other parents with unvoiced questions in the air. Was this 'bad parenting'? Were they 'bad parents'? Meanwhile the child grew in confidence and independence.

As children, the school took us on a nature walk each week.

More focus on the whole child's development is needed – including socialising, sport, art, music; exams to be reduced significantly. A primary school teacher told me the other day he felt the government was now regretting introducing SATs but he felt they were now stuck with them. My own efforts have paid off with my son. He is a delightful, mature, playful child. I have restricted his access to video, TV and sweets, etc. It's sad to hear his peers mumbling incoherently. He will be increasingly exposed to his peers and peer-culture and I am not sure exactly what I will do about that when the time comes. However, if his first five years have limited the more harmful elements, I think that will put him in good stead (and of course – most importantly – his secure relationship with me.)

Nurturing a love of learning can be helped by cultivating a love and respect for books and stories; by going to museums if practical and especially the use of the public library. With regard to learning to read, not worrying if a child won't read a book but by providing comics, acknowledging that it is cultivating a love of books and reading.

We should learn from children instead of always expecting them to learn from us.

Children are not perks to be exhibited as successful competitors in the great educational brain race. They are the continuation of the human race and the qualities they imbibe as children are the qualities that will show through in the society of the future.

Try to see your child's first teacher at nursery or primary school a week or so after they start – no other reason than to introduce yourself and get a basic understanding of the person in charge of your child. You will then have a framework of reference when your child talks of his school day. It will also help the teacher to understand your child if you describe what kind of a nature they have.

Teachers are expected to chart the intellectual growth of your child within rather strict yearly boundaries of achievement from a very early age (government policy.) But unfortunately they all have their own growing spurts. Try to relax and not worry if they have not learnt to read at an early age. Children at Rudolf Steiner Schools are not taught to read and write until the age of seven but then easily pick up the skill, without all the sense of failure and pressure so often associated with peer group pressure.

If you do have the time, volunteer to help in your child's class in a regular slot, if only for a term. It may just be two hours one afternoon a week but the experience can be invaluable in understanding your child and their friends and to get a balanced view of any difficulties or behaviour problems that are emerging. Schools can be large and quite harsh environments. Just your presence and show of interest can be enough to help the child settle and adapt.

If, and it may not be possible, you can allow them a day off when they look really peaky, it can just be enough to stop them getting ill and bring their energy levels back. It does not produce a drop-out attitude but actually shows that you respect the signs of exhaustion and they can relax knowing that someone is watching out for them. Take the time to re-mind them of personal care and love.

If they don't want to go to school, you can simply explain that the land we live in has laws. If you explain that it is not up to you, it will be harder to see you as an unreasonable being. It also teaches them that there are greater powers than that of the parent – an introduction to a larger society.

I work for a voluntary organisation called Springbound that helps deprived children who have missed out on learning to read – which should be the right of every child. Teachers are so inundated with work that they cannot possibly give individual attention to each child. So we are given training in basic phonics hoping to make a breakthrough so that they will overcome their problems, but we must not see it as the one single way of teaching every child to read.

My six year old daughter was bullied by a boy in her class. It was in the playground and the teacher in charge did not see what happened until she was knocked to the ground and trying to hit him off with blows using feet and arms. They were both punished for fighting. After meetings with the head teacher and the Board of Governors justice was finally achieved. There should be much more supervision in the playground, with assistant teachers and trained older pupils playing their part.

We have a lot of pressure to get our young children's play to be instructive. I just want to have fun with them.

Schools have not necessarily much to do with education…they are mainly institutions of control where certain basic habits must be instilled in the young. Education is different and has little place in school. *Winston Churchill*

Chapter 9
Positive Behaviour

"Be kind wherever possible… it is always possible." His Holiness the Dalai Lama

The most important thing about behaviour is to recognise that all children want boundaries, although this is not always apparent. Boundaries are lines of demarcation about how far they can go and, if they don't know, they will push their behaviour to the utmost to find out at what stage it will not be tolerated. They need to be reassured that their parents are in control and not them. By concentrating on the younger age groups in every sphere of life, there is no doubt that we can make a difference to their well-being in their teenage years and beyond. The rise in the number of teenagers with behavioural problems and suffering from anxiety and depression is well documented. There has also been a dramatic rise in the incidence of attention-deficit problems, violence, eating disorders, binge drinking and other addictions.

Children need to understand that the boundaries that are laid down are for good reasons: their security and well-being and also social consideration, and these can be explained to them even at a young age. As they grow older, the rules will have to be continually adjusted, but the principle of keeping to the boundaries remains the same. Also they can take an ever greater part in agreeing and even initiating these boundaries. If they are kept as few and as simple as possible, there is more chance of them being kept as a matter of course and, as usual, the earlier the routine the better.

What about enforcing these agreed rules of conduct? Should there be sanctions? Each family will have ideas about this, but as a general rule, the principle of 'cause and effect' is a pointer, or in the old fashioned saying, "Let the punishment fit the crime". Young children are much more able to get the gist of logic than we give them credit for; they understand that if they spoil something belonging to someone else they should make amends in some way; or if they get up too late in the morning then they need to go to sleep earlier.

I know that it is not that simple, but the overall factor in establishing rules is that they are carried out with love and mutual respect. You still love them, but you don't love what they have done. This makes all the difference in the world. It is not easy for parents to cast off the punitive shackles of the Victorian age and yet still maintain firm boundaries. The days of, "Wait till your dad comes home, he'll get his belt out," are mercifully diminishing. In fact, the disciplinary rôle of the father has sometimes been undermined by a growing tendency, on the part of both parents, to defend their offspring even when they are in the wrong.

The debate as to whether or not to use physical punishment is still rampant and I come down firmly on the principle of never using physical force. Finally the use of the cane or any kind of physical punishment has been banned in schools. It certainly took a long and bitter struggle to get Britain to conform to the European ruling – finally being defeated at the European Court of Justice.

So now the arguments are most active on the question of whether or not parents should smack their children; "Just a small tap on the hand" is the case put forward. The most valid point against inflicting any physical pain, however mild, is that all young children imitate and take their parents as rôle models for their actions and their values. So the message they receive is that hitting is permitted when someone is not doing what they should. This can be a double standard, as they may be told not to hit members of their family or their playmates, even if they are hit first. Television and computer games also convey the message that they would have received from being smacked: that 'might is right'. So in a world which should not and dare not resort to violence to solve its problems, we need future citizens who will negotiate rather than be precipitated into war.

But it can be said that this is literally world's away from the little tap on the hand, often used to teach children to protect themselves. Maybe, but why not hold them firmly if it is necessary to protect them from danger and, at the same time, gradually train them to avoid danger while seeing that they are not exposed to it wherever possible.

There is considerable research showing how often physical punishment has to be repeated, probably with increased vigour. In schools, the caning books bore testimony to the continual 'recidivists' before it was banned; and in the same way parents have found that smacking can finally become ineffective.

So I strongly oppose any form of physical punishment being inflicted on the young – and on the adults for that matter. As the parent is bigger and stronger than the offspring, it has traces of bullying. It is noteworthy that when the child is bigger and probably stronger than the parent it will stop, if not before!

The debate continues; a quick smack does not drag on as other punishments might, but then this could be administered in anger, which is not good role-modelling. If on the other hand, it is carried out coldly at a specified time, it could have a sadistic or, at least, a self-righteous flavour, "This hurts me more than it hurts you!" Neither approach is good parenting.

A final point against physical punishment is that the infliction of pain can reduce the respect that should be a mutual factor of the parent-child relationship and this also applies to the teacher-pupil relationship. This does not alter the fact that both parents and teachers are responsible for the boundaries which need to be complied with. With mutual respect, children can understand that it is their behaviour that needs correction and that they are appreciated and loved for their own sake.

With physical punishment not being an option, the opinions of parents and teachers will vary as to whether to apply actual sanctions or to spend time discussing any misdemeanours, or both. 'Time out' has been widely discussed and, if it is interpreted as taking a space of time to be still and contemplate what has happened, this can be very helpful, although time is not always on our side. At home, it can be counterproductive if it is demeaning, like standing in the 'punishment corner', or it can be a happy release such as being sent to one's room where there is a multitude of toys to play with. The best way that parents can encourage children to reflect on their misdemeanours is to stay quietly with the culprit and then talk about what has happened.

For teachers, this solution is even less realisable with over thirty pupils in a class and limited 'free time'. Still, teachers often do manage to discuss bad behaviour with individuals and this can pay dividends, especially if there is extra help in the classroom. Also there are many schools that have trained older pupils, some as young as eight-years-old, to mediate in disruptive disputes, especially in the playground. These young mentors have proved to be successful in helping to control the increasing threat of bullying. Together with a really strong school policy of zero tolerance these practices can make it much more difficult for bullies to operate in secrecy. Another relatively new approach has been to change the attitude of bystanders which is a key factor in research from Canada. This found that 75 per cent of peer interventions in bullying incidents were successful with the slogan: "Bullying: See it. Get help. Stop it."

A favourite approach in dealing with behaviour in the home and at school is by rewards for good conduct and vice versa. These can take the form of stars, achievement on notice boards, announcements etc. and can be very effective and, even with no equivalents for bad behaviour, the very fact that a star isn't won can be a stigma. In any case, good behaviour needs to be recognised and affirmed. What can happen, however, is that the children become dependent on their adults' approval to the extent that their own self-regulation is impaired. We all want our children to become self-governing and self-sufficient as we steer the delicate course between using our position of authority and letting go.

Behaviour is all about good relationships and having consideration for others and, if we can have this perspective together with firm boundaries and respect, we will have done our best and our children will be more likely to do theirs. It is all a question of balance.

Parents' contributions

Early intervention is the key to establishing good behaviour patterns. We started making the boundaries clear from the beginning with mutual respect as the keynote. This seems much better than a punitive approach later on, such as compulsory parenting classes or jail for the parents whose children are persistent truants.

If you try to hide strong emotions, your behaviour will still communicate something to a child and they may wrongly believe that they are to blame. Let them know if you are worried or irritable and tell them that you may be a bit snappy or bad tempered for a while and it is not their fault. If it is their behaviour that is distressful, try to address the problem as soon as possible, before tension really builds up, making sure that they know it is not them but their behaviour that disturbs you.

When my children are sufficiently agitated that they begin to lose control over their behaviour, I ask them to walk across the length of the house to the red couch, turn clockwise three times and anticlockwise three times, and return to me. In my experience, the attention needed to follow that direction changes or redirects their thought process so that when they return they are in some way changed. This serves several aims – to know that feelings can be changed through how we move our body, to treat even a child's unskillful behaviour with dignity, and to make changing how we behave simple and easy, not a cause for abuse.

Another tool I use is a taking time out rather than giving a time out – though not in the way one might expect. If I feel I am losing patience or myself becoming agitated, I take a time out. I say "I am taking a time out and I will be back when I feel calm again" and I leave the room. When I have had time to settle myself I return. I find that it is much more powerful to a child to remove oneself than to remove a child, in part because it is unexpected. One circumvents possible power struggles when one takes accountability first for one's self. My children are able now to take time outs when it would be of benefit to them.

In my son's school, there are older pupils specially trained by Childline to help stop bullying. They are popular and seem to get results. It stops me worrying about whether he might be being bullied.

Children are to be treated with respect and as having much greater capabilities mentally and socially than are attributed to them.

Where discipline is concerned, the view of my two daughters differs somewhat and I am waiting to see the results of the two approaches. The elder relies entirely on the authority of herself and her husband and the child's own self-discipline and motivation. They neither punish nor reward. They have read that this intrinsic discipline is more effective than anything which is externally imposed. This approach seems to be working well: the children seem healthy, happy, sociable, reasonably behaved and doing well at school.

The other daughter and her husband operate along similar lines but sometimes they use 'extrinsic methods'. For instance, their son, as he vigorously resists eating anything but a very restricted diet, is rewarded with a star for trying something different and is now eating much more varied food. Also they have taken to giving yellow and red cards! This works very well and only one red card has ever had to be awarded! The awareness that these sanctions may be used seems to be enough. The method has helped with an unruly phase, which was perhaps due to the inevitable difficulties of having only one child in the family. The different systems may well reflect the varied temperaments of parents and children. Flexibility is vital.

These ideas are not new or startling. I have realised it is more a question of getting back to old ways which are still valid and effective even in today's changed circumstances.

Positive behaviour is something that has to be encouraged and rewarded. It is something that has to be acknowledged also. A 'good' child is often overlooked, whereas a 'negative' child often achieves more attention. The pros and cons of positive behaviour, as opposed to negative behaviour, have to be made clear to the child, e.g. doing homework without a fuss may result in a treat. Negative behaviour – swearing – results in alienation and anger.

The only big problem that I have, through my own thoughtlessness, is to do all the jobs around the house myself for speed etc. when I should have made the time to include the family in the chores. I find myself moaning at them now that they are old enough to help but have not the habit and I can't expect them to suddenly realise what needs being done. I wish I had made them feel that it was normal to help me and my husband from a very young age.

Most children love to help! So helping adults through their own example of doing meaningful work delights many children. This work can be cleaning, looking after younger children and pets, gardening, cooking, woodwork, making baskets, weaving and spinning, making yoghurt and cheese, growing indoor sprouts and greens, charity work and hospital visiting, learning how to care for a hive of bees – the list is endless. Meaningful work in the world is an endless task, needing to be brought into the here and now, every day, with our children. This work can become play too if we go about every task with a joyful heart. What is important is our example to our children – the way we present experiences to them is the way they will imitate. So we need to be positive, loving and joyful about everything we do for, or with, our children.

As adults, we must listen more carefully and more imaginatively to what children are saying about the world they live in and have the confidence to take responsibility for acting on what they have to say, whilst correcting and supporting them when we need to.

If we expose our children to adult fears – fears that they have no ability to do anything about – we cripple them and cow their enthusiasm to learn on a simple level. They need to learn simple ideas to start with, so that more complex ideas can be comprehended later on. It is not just maths that has to be staged as building blocks. Children often find exposure to the daily negative and sensational news on television more frightening than films that contain violence but have a beginning and an end and can be comprehended in terms of right and wrong (one hopes!).

When I watch those programmes about little children being completely out of control and the psychologist or 'Super Nanny' being called in to take over, I feel that parenting is being marginalised. These are extremes, which make a sensation, but many of us are 'good enough' and are coping reasonably well. Of course, there are behaviour problems and I find the best thing with my three-year-old is to try to spend a quiet time together, holding her, if necessary.

I have just begun requiring my children to each do two chores each day – little helping things like putting away cutlery, hanging up washing, unloading the washing machine, distributing clean laundry to people's bedrooms etc. My son is learning how to make his own bed and peg up socks. After they have completed their two allocated jobs, they can choose to do extra things to help for which they can claim a shiny 2p for their money box. The idea is to engender responsible attitudes, willing work and taking pride in doing something well and developing life skills. They realise that some things are hard work and that you have to persevere in order to finish, and not everything is what you feel like doing at the time. It is also fun working together and satisfying seeing a job completed, and counting up the rewards of your labours.

I feel my children should be interested in someone else's life. There is always something to learn. We have a friend, an old lady from Church who is in her eighties, who comes to stay sometimes. She likes being with a family and is a pleasure to have and full of interesting sayings and stories. We want our children to love and relate to people of all ages.

Take your children regularly, if possible, to meet someone from an older generation. Why not get them to make a card, or pick some flowers and tie them up to give as a present – or a homemade gift or painting from school? Grandparents are often indulgent to their grand-children and this would establish an understanding of reciprocation or just the joy of giving.

The new baby will be every bit as intricate as its parents, but at the start it is helpless, defenceless, without knowledge of the society he or she has been born into but with a fundamental urge to learn and survive by mimicry and pattern itself on those that are in close proximity and a position of care. (It is interesting to note those few known cases of 'wild children' brought up by animals who mimic the behaviour completely of their 'foster parents'.)

Whether you know it or not, your behaviour will be responsible for that early patterning – even by your absence or who you choose to look after your child; your attitude and unvoiced tensions and moments of relaxation and happiness all feed in to this physically, mentally and spiritually thirsty little being. A baby literally sucks up everything during its waking hours and processes its newly-gained wisdom while sleeping.

If my children misbehaved, I would simply grip their forearm firmly and they would stop.

When my daughter was five or six, she loved playing alone in her room. If I needed to speak to her, I would knock on her door, respecting her space.

A child is not better or worse as a person because he can or cannot do long division or has a high or low IQ or gets into trouble. Thus, to see young people merely as members of categories is to fail to respect them as persons.

The capacity for respecting others in later life derives in great measure from the experience in childhood of being respected for what one is, not only for what one does. Such unconditional respect helps young people to gain self-respect, which in turn is conducive to respecting others – a virtuous circle.

We agreed not to say, "No!" to them but to try and distract them from what they are doing.

Since our son has taken up martial arts, he has gained a lot of confidence.

Our school has started yoga as part of the curriculum and it is a great success.

There is no such thing as a bad child, only a 'sad' child. How true.

Chapter 10
Keeping Technology Under Control

For tribal man space was the uncontrollable mystery: for technological man it is time that occupies the same role.
Marshall McLuhan

Nowhere has the revolution in material goods been more welcome than in catering for household needs. Hot and cold water to hand on the turning of a tap, central heating, dish washers and washing machines have all eliminated the drudgery experienced during much of the 20th Century. Parents have had extra bonuses with disposable nappies and collapsible push-chairs. This is progress and no one would want to put that clock back.

Now, innovation in technology has been bursting at the seams, especially during the last decade, and there is much more to come. It is the pace of change that has been phenomenal. To quote Sue Palmer, "In less than two decades, technology has transformed our homes: PCs, laptops, email, the worldwide web; cable, satellite and digital TV, camcorders, DVD, computer games, play stations, pods, mobile phones, text messaging, camphones. And everything happens much, much faster than it did in the past". Sue Palmer, *Toxic Childhood*, 2006.

At the advent of the Industrial Revolution the Luddites blamed the machines and sought to destroy them because of the exploitation of labour, including young children, and all that that entailed. Likewise, today there are some parents who would put the whole blame on television when their children become addicted.

It is, of course, the use, or rather the misuse, of television that causes the trouble. There is so much of value for children in the judicious enjoyment of television and the internet: it widens their horizons in many spheres, for example the wonders of the natural world, and there is good entertainment when they can just relax during their hurried lives. For young children much depends on guidance and selection by the adults in charge and many programmes can be an inspiration for their imaginative creative play. Soon they will be initiated into choosing their favourite programmes, always with a limit on the time spent, and where possible the adult in charge will watch with them and discuss what they have seen. Children who are used to choosing what they prefer are more likely to be self-regulating and be less content with the endless parade of 'goodies' and 'baddies' trying to eliminate each other.

Having painted an ideal picture of discriminating parents watching their children's choice with them, we mustn't underestimate the power of the media, especially of television, where the marketers aim to capture young viewers by all means possible. They are well aware that children can be deeply influenced by ads and brand names and they have the audacity to press their gullible audience to pester their parents to buy, buy, buy! In fact advertisers spend millions targeting the very young, including those under two years old. In the US, research has shown that, following a drive to imprint brand names on their minds, the sales of the particular commodity went up by 30 per cent. And British marketers are not far behind.

We should be aware of neuro-marketing – the study of the brain while exposed to marketing messages – which is now a billion dollar advertising business. It provides a way of measuring which brands get remembered and these will then be specially promoted. A study by the Centre for Cognitive Liberty and Ethics argues that it is unethical to use neuro-marketing for children's products. However the advertising industry in the US is reckoned to spend $10 billion on neuro-marketing trying to find out whether or not ads are effective. As they spend $100 billion plus in the media, they want to measure if their message is being recognized. In Britain there is a strong lobby calling for no advertising in children's programmes and the practice of neuro-marketing makes this legislation even more vital.

It is the 'must have' syndrome that marketers cultivate: collectibles for doll's sets for the girls and deadly military equipment for the boys and the very latest CDs and mobiles for both. For the billion pound advertising industry, 'new' is the operative word and goods are almost obsolete by the time they reach the market. Since technology develops at breakneck speed, it is easy to persuade the public to keep up-to-date with the very latest innovations and children are well aware of the kudos that this bestows.

Computer games can have the same attraction as spending hours glued to the television. Both have the deserved reputation of containing far too much violence and computer games can be mesmerisingly addictive. The purveyors of TV programmes and computer games go to great lengths to assert that the violence has no effect on children unless they are clinically disturbed. But this argument is contradicted by the fact that all television is calculated to have considerable influence on viewers – which is why enormous sums of money are spent on advertising.

There is also considerable evidence to show that too much violence has a desensitizing effect, apart from the dubious values of maintaining that 'might' is the solution in the defence of 'right'.

Another important reason for limiting young children's viewing is that they do not find it easy to differentiate between fact and fantasy, so it can be that much harder to cope with fiction that manifests itself as frighteningly real. It is also true that exposure to the daily grind of news programmes can have a devastating effect, promulgating fear.

The expression 'happy medium' can well be targeted at the excessive use of television and computer games and it has already been pointed out that too much can impoverish family life and greatly impair physical well-being. In a 2006 Portuguese study of 3,000 children between the ages of seven and nine, it was found that prolonged television-watching was associated with an increased risk of obesity. Moreover, it is the overall negative picture of life so often portrayed by the media that can be harmful to children

The 'happy medium' approach can also be applied to the internet, which is a keen competitor with television and apparently winning more audiences with its participatory approach. This is undoubtedly the doorway to the outer world and its use can be a great source of information, stimulation, creativity and, especially, communication. With the computer, greetings can be illustrated in the form of original artwork which can be really creative. Our youngsters put us to shame with their immediate grasp of its intricacies: they can visit the great unknown, practice a new form of art and make contact with new friends in faraway places. This availability of the unknown also has its dangers, so parents need to be extra vigilant in monitoring their offspring, who can be gullible in the extreme.

Another miraculous invention that has played a major part in children's lives is the mobile phone: now they can speak to relations and friends anywhere in the world with the possibility of sharing a video picture of themselves into the bargain. The extensive use of mobiles can have a good effect on their communication skills, especially if there are difficulties about face-to-face talk, through shyness or distance. Texting, being speedy, cheaper and less exposing, has overtaken the spoken word.

However, the new gadgets cannot take the place of face-to-face contact, although they might be quicker and more convenient.

There is still a valuable place for letters and greetings, handwritten and possibly with paintings or drawings to illustrate them. It may be slower and looked down upon, as the term 'snail mail' suggests, but it can give great pleasure to the recipient and to the writer/artist alike.

The downside for parents of the use of mobiles is that although they allow their children to be in touch when venturing out, there is a great risk of their being stolen or children being bullied into handing them over. Schools have increasingly banned their use and parents should resist giving them to pre-teenagers and at that stage, investigate the possibility of using models that are able to be legally traced.

With the rapid expansion of mobiles capable of multiple-use, parents need to be aware of sites on the internet which encourage the display of dubious and often violent videos filmed on mobile phones. These encourage comments, sometimes of a racist nature, and sometimes with an audience of spectators enthusiastically condoning the violence.

Finally, we must ask what are the effects of electro-magnetic fields on the nervous system of young children sitting in front of computer screens? There can be no long-term research at present as computer use is still in its infancy. A similar question mark hangs over the excessive use of mobile phones and there is also a growing concern over the proliferation of radio masts.

Parents' contributions

I think television is a tricky one for many parents today. Now many children have a television and a computer in their rooms. I personally disagree with that. I feel that young children cannot and should not be made responsible for monitoring what they watch and for how long. Too much television leaves no room for much else, like reading and personal communication.

Ultimately a parent should monitor what is on television. I can remember not letting them watch Grange Hill and them wanting to. One day, I thought "How can I make a judgment on a programme I haven't watched?" I did watch it and found that all the episodes had a moral and after that my children watched it.

A male colleague from work – his contribution about television. He lets his fifteen year old daughter have a television in her room and trusts that after nine pm she doesn't watch it. He said as a child, he had to watch what his parents watched and hated it. He feels that modern children know so much anyway and that you can't really stop them.

We appreciate the best of what television has to offer our young: widening their horizons and getting a perspective of the world we live in, not only the disasters, but the sheer wonder at the many-faceted delights of nature.

There are wonderful things to explore from the burgeoning electronic industry. We must always bear in mind that these inventions are neither good nor bad; they are neutral, being entirely dependent on the human condition, in other words, what we make of it. For example, there is a range of creativity that can emanate from the use of the computer: in music one's talents can be exercised in many variations: artistic ability can be developed through colour, shape etc.; and the playing of instruments can be explored by merging with other musical programmes, thus enlarging one's horizons. So the positive side of all of these innovations can be explored in order to enlarge one's capabilities – which should be continually acknowledged and encouraged throughout childhood.

Resisting the enticements of the electronic industry: television, computer games, mobiles, internet; with all of these it is important to have a carefully managed approach. Television could be kept for a later date, at least for the first born, with habits already formed to do other natural things such as a variety of sports: swimming, walking in the countryside. The principle is not dissimilar to the age-old practice of diverting children when they are fractious: an enticing change soon captures their attention. Similarly, if children are used to enjoyable alternatives to watching TV or playing computer games, they will be less likely to forsake them for more passive entertainment.

However, for most parents there has to be a compromise and there our guidance plays a big part. As soon as the TV plays a role then we can watch chosen programmes together and if there seems to be a very limited choice, there are excellent DVDs.

I feel strongly that all access to technology – TV and computer access – should be monitored and controlled with regard to children and young people.

Television does dominate present day life and many of the programmes are not desirable influences on young minds being brought up according to these values. Therefore the television is not in the bedroom but in the living room where parents can monitor what is being watched. This does not necessarily mean forbidding certain programmes so much as discussing undesirable aspects with the children so that they learn not to accept everything they see unquestioningly.

Every afternoon after school Sam doesn't turn the TV on when he gets home. He rushes along to his desk, which is in the living room downstairs near where everyone is moving about, and makes rockets, whales, trees, all sorts of things and he writes. He likes his 'inventions' – spacecraft etc.

At our children's school, they are involved in film-making. The pupils choose the topic and do the research and then co-operate in creating it from start to finish. I think this is a great way to prepare them for a media–rich future. It will help them to discriminate between the immense volume of the media resources offered to them.

There is an onslaught of high pressure, interactive modes of technology, texting and messages on sites such as Facebook and Bebo, which are also contributing to the stress affecting young people. They could be getting twenty messages a day and spending hours in front of a screen. They can be aware of the outer world but not aware of themselves.

It is good that the kids work together on computer games and that they can talk to people all over the world, but they do spend too much time on them and this isn't good for their physical health.

There has to be a balance between texting and writing which could be developed into creative expression in original stories and poems. My children have made their own booklets, 'publishing' their efforts.

Why can't there be ratings for TV and computer games like we have for films; also easier ways of blocking undesirable programmes?

My eight-year-old daughter is far more disturbed by violence seen on the news than in fictional programmes.

Many intelligent women I meet believe their very young children's dexterity with computers – learning numbers, colours etc. (three year olds) is advancing their development; they are very proud that their three and four year-olds know their way around a computer. (I myself am singularly unimpressed and nonchalant/puzzled about this 'pride' about something so stupid and unworthy.) This is the case – even when their children are backward – re. talking, socially etc. I could recount some wonderful conversations on this matter.

Such parents have been misled by advertisers and 'educators' that this is 'advancement' and this needs to be corrected. My local school teaches computer-use to four and five year-olds and all schools have computer rooms whilst their play areas and sports facilities are pitiful. (The same goes for schools that spend £1,000s on computers but children are educationally, totally neglected.)

As well as ignorance, competitiveness (parents do seem more competitive even about their very young children) is at the heart of it; that their children will not succeed in SATs etc, that they will be left behind, and that their children need to 'prove' their brightness and precociousness in this way to their parents!

We have acquired two rabbits as pets and the children helped their dad build the hutch, designing it first on the computer. They have their own computer, as an aid to their schoolwork, and because it is important for them to acquire proficiency at school. Both are adept with a range of software and my daughter at six years old can use a desktop publishing package to produce leaflets, posters and cards independently and design web-site pages (not linked to anything at present)!

They use the internet on their dad's office computer and theirs will also be connected when our friend can come and sort it out for us. Their computer is situated in the kitchen near their schoolwork area so that I can try and help and so that we are aware of what they are accessing. They each have a stereo in their room; we don't have TV but are not in favour of TVs or computers in bedrooms. The computer is a mixed blessing because the children love using it and it can be anti-social. I try not to let them use the computer or watch videos when other children are visiting but find that visiting children are often more than willing to engage in less participative parallel play – being 'shown' something on the computer.

Watching DVDs and videos is a tool and we relax and enjoy but we discourage the children from passively imbibing. We pause and ask questions; we ask for our children's opinions and perceptions and have been amazed at what they have taken in. We want our children to consider: "Is that true? Did that really happen? Was that a good thing to do? How did that make you feel?" We are giving our children a glimpse of past and present and the vast wonderful world they live in and from a safe and familiar place let them see the side of life that isn't good and talk about why. My daughter notices discrepancies in story CDs or where a story has been abridged. She criticises illustrations in books – "He wouldn't have looked like that because…"

We went to the Mining Museum in Keswick and the lady enthused about what we would see adding "And there's a video with accounts of people who used to work in the mines, but the children won't be interested in that…" They watched twenty minutes of it before asking to move on and were very interested and of course, I had to answer a lot of "You know the bit where (such and such)…but why mummy?"

I was brought up with no TV or video, so read extensively; my husband had TV and loves it. We read a marriage book when we were engaged with what we felt was wise advice – that it was good not to have a TV in the first year of marriage in order to develop communication with each other. We have been married nine years now and have never felt the need to get a TV. When we've had one on holiday, we've flicked channels, found nothing much that was worth watching but ended up watching it anyway and felt robbed of our time.

Television is seen as a demon and there is no doubt that it has an effect on young lives. But it is the demon we love and have become addicted to. How else can a mother cope sometimes – if there is no close extended family, no money for clubs and home-help and the need to recoup her own energy for the next day's work? (Young children, it has to be said, can be very boring, particularly when they are not a shared responsibility.) Recognise your limits. But try to relax and sit with them while watching; make it a shared experience. You will then have a much better idea of the effect it has and what they watch – and you can make comments or change the channel. They can share a parallel real world rather than be lost in the box.

I found that the book "The Media Diet for Kids" by Teresa Orange and Louise O'Flynn very helpful in getting that happy medium in regulating my children's TV and Internet time.

Sitting in front of a computer screen does not help a child develop and learn how to manipulate the world they live in. If you want your child to learn and to grow, give them your time and read stories, engage them in dramatic play and build things with blocks, etc. Don't bother with all the games marketed to accelerate your pre-schoolers' learning; reading with your child and talking back and forth about things in the story gives the stimulation they need.

I feel that the biggest influence is their peers: kids want the very latest computer games because their mates have got it or are going to get it. They want the latest thing advertised on TV. We give so much pocket money and they can work out for themselves what they can afford – we can't but we often end up giving nothing of ourselves which is what they really want.

Chapter 11
What Values Do We Choose?

You cannot teach a man anything.
You can only help him discover it within himself.
Galileo Galilei

All parents wish to give their children a deep sense of the value system that they themselves embrace and even if this not articulated they want their children to value themselves and others. It is often said that it is not possible to value others if you do not value yourself, and the basic gift that we can bestow on our children is one of a good self-concept and self-respect.

Where do they get their values from? The overwhelming source is from us, their parents, and it is quite awesome to realise how much they will model themselves on the values that we portray. We all know that children are the world's best imitators and it is disconcerting to know that they are only too well aware of our imperfections. For example, we want our children to be truthful and honest and here we are often put to the test as models, when in a busy life we resort to 'white lies': "Tell them I'm out" to an unwelcome caller, where the message could easily be modified into the truth that we are too tired or too busy. Here the value of respect for others plays a great part; parents and children alike have to learn to be skilful in not hurting feelings while sticking to the truth. Children have a head-start in that they are basically honest and this needs to be nourished.

Cooperation is certainly a value that we would wish for our children. Good relationships are all important, from toddlerhood where learning to share and to play together is the beginning of a long learning process. In our present society the emphasis is all on competition, but the strong desire to be the winner has to be tempered with consideration for others. Closely related to cooperation is compassion which is about seeing the others' point of view and empathising with them. Besides being the essential ingredient in good relationships, it is vital in the resolution of conflicts.

In an increasingly turbulent world, the value of being peaceful ranks high; it incorporates stillness and peace of mind as well as the ability to solve any conflicts without having recourse to fighting back – no easy task in the crowded playground.

A virtue which is struggling to survive in modern day life is that of simplicity, but its worth is becoming more apparent as parents grapple with the consumer society. It could be a goal to aim at; more tranquility instead of 'overload'.

In all of these attributes that we wish for our children, we can only be good role models if we promote them actively; if we walk our talk. Young children's learning is largely through action and so their values are largely formed by doing, as well as by observing others.

A great boost to children being valued is that at last they have their own charter of human rights under the auspices of the United Nations. If they are valued for their own sake and not treated as second-class citizens – or not even citizens – then they are more likely to respect the rights of others. It is worth emphasising that rights are automatically matched with responsibilities for adults and children alike, and that respect is the keynote in all relationships when rights and duties are measured. There is a lobby that blames these acquired rights for the increase in young people's bad behaviour, whereas much of the trouble is the continuing lack of respect and trust in them.

But how true it is that 'no man is an island' and nowhere in history have there been such powerful influences from outside the home; this has an enormous effect on the values that we all pick up and children are especially vulnerable in this respect. The media is the mouthpiece of the consumer society and as we have seen in the last chapter, its values are made clear though the press and the latest innovations in technology.

Probably the single most pervasive influence on children is the value attached to material possessions: trainers, toys, clothes, toiletries – all in line with the throw-away concept with the word 'new' as the essential element. But these are relatively small-fry compared with the compulsion to possess the very latest invention in technology: MP3 players, digital cameras, mobile phones, computers, TV, DVDs, with their accompanying software. The mania to buy is a really big problem for parents; their children can be made to feel inferior by their peers if they haven't the latest gear with brand names, the latest CDs, DVDs and the latest hardware at home. This state of affairs can create an atmosphere of need on the part of the children and in some cases can lead to verbal and even physical bullying at school if their needs are not met. Many parents feel that they have to comply with consumerism in order for their children to be in the swim and for the great majority it is impossible to supply the ever-increasing demand. Even relatively well-off parents have come to dread the demands for birthday parties which have to be 'out of this world' with regard to entertainers or fashionable venues, let alone compulsory party bags of presents.

This raises the question of the role in children's lives of the cult of the personality. This emphasis on 'celebrities with everything' on television leads to aspirations towards being famous and some parents are pressed to make their children's dreams of fame come true. Sometimes the parents themselves are the ambitious instigators of these dreams of stardom for their young: little aspiring dancers or singers are put through the mill of intensive training, which has little to do with creative enjoyment.

In a highly competitive world there are few who can reach the top, leaving a trail of disappointed 'failures'. So the final high flyers are often esteemed as role models for their countless admirers; winners of contests, footballers and especially pop stars. But are their roles always good ones to follow? Apart from the use of dubious means to reach the top, their conduct is not always to be admired: abuse of drugs and alcohol, violence and cheating on the football field are the most publicised, but a more subtle influence, like the full endorsement of the competitive society which has brought them success, can be much more insidious. However, we must not forget the celebrities and stars who our children could do well to emulate; for example, those who devote their support to the poorest nations or to the caring for the environment.

Another considerable influence through the media is the cult of fashion and this is closely related to the aspirations of the young. Of course, there has always been great publicity in the fashion field, but never before has it been so accessible to the very young. There has always been dressing up with mothers' dance frocks or ball-gowns and impossibly high-heeled shoes, but today it is more for real, even to the extent of designer labels being 'a must'. Girls have been the main targets in the past and now it is not only their own clothes but also those of their sophisticated dolls – and boys are getting just as fashion-conscious. This targeting of younger and younger children creates the desire in them to grow up more quickly than ever before.

Our society is basically competitive and this is reflected in the many television programmes that feature knock-out competitions for aspirant stars with the audience experiencing apparent empathy with the losers as one by one they are gradually eliminated. Is it empathy or is there an element of voyeurism, seeing through the compulsory stiff upper lip to another's distress of losing? The purveyors of such highly profitable programmes always state that it is essential to learn to be good losers in a naturally competitive society. There is certainly ample opportunity to learn this lesson publicly in everyday life.

This exploration of some of the values that come over loud and clear in the media may be criticised as seeing dangers in programmes that are purely fun and good entertainment. This is true for each individual programme; but their profusion, whether of violence, knock-out competitions, or high-powered consumer promotion, adds up to an entrenched system of values for the children that imbibe them. The inevitable defence is that they do not need to watch so much and it is the parents' responsibility to ensure that they do not misuse the media, but it is also the responsibility of the programme makers.

This is a small sample of values that parents might aspire to; they will obviously have their own choices and these will not always be those that underlie the messages conveyed in our society. So there will be role models that our children will be inclined to emulate; for example, pop stars and footballers. Sometimes they can encourage the public to give help to others who are suffering, but more often the message is insidious – the supreme importance of material acquisitions and personal glamour – and this chimes with the aspirations of young children, and especially 'teenagers', to grow up quickly and sample all these goodies.

So parents have an uphill task, especially if their own aspirations do not coincide with current trends. However, we must not get the whole picture out of proportion; a lot of the innovations and glamour can be fun. It is like everything else – one has to achieve the happy medium.

Parents' contributions

A very important fact for me to is that for a holistic childhood, parents need to give examples in their own behaviour. I have learnt so much about my own and how it affects my children. I have constantly to remind myself to strive to give good examples to children of how to live and communicate and express themselves.

As a young child I was read Aesop's Fables and Greek Myths. I always loved the stories and characters but something that stuck with me was the morals the stories carried; for example, the story of King Midas who asked the gods to give him the power to turn everything he touched into gold. Although at first he was delighted with what he thought of as a blessing, he soon found it to be more of a curse as he could neither eat nor drink nor touch his family and those he loved without them turning to gold. Thinking about this story now I believe it taught me that gold and money are not as important as food, drink and people. Now, at nineteen years-old, I have no desire to be extremely rich but simply to be comfortable. I think these stories carry important messages and morals that children take on subconsciously and which then affect them in later life.

Values chosen are different for all of us as it is not only from our childhood environment but also from what we see going on around us; how we are treated personally; how we view the double standards of the world; how much corruption we may experience as children and adults; and what values are given to us as part of our inheritance in a family. All this will determine the sort of values we pass on to our children. My own daughter now has a daughter and feels very much that I, as a mother, imparted good values to her that she in turn is passing on to her child.

WHAT VALUES DO WE CHOOSE?

If we involve our children in decision-making it will help them to sort out what they feel is right.

John can be bribed to behave himself or get his schoolwork done with the promise of a toy. He is not given things like mobile phones etc as some are. Some of his classmates have more of an idea of what is 'fashionable' than he does; he is not like that at all.

Honouring and respecting whatever a child creates, rather than assessing and judging – asking the child what he/she is expressing rather than imposing interpretations. This is a parallel with therapy and the therapeutic relationship; taking the risk of being oneself and their feeling 'at home' with that. The adventurous snail – the slightest touch sends it back into its shell.

I found that inundating children with toys can have an adverse effect. They get overwhelmed and over-stimulated and cannot concentrate on any one thing long enough or on any one thing to learn from it so they just shut down. They are not learning to play imaginatively either. I feel that it can restrict their development and may even harm children.

'Expensive hi-tech toys are a waste of money – children learn just as much from playing with an old mobile phone'. Keep it simple. A nursery was persuaded to pack away all playthings for three months leaving only tables, chairs, blankets and their own initiative. After a day of boredom the children had turned tables and blankets into dens and were absorbed in make-believe games. They became more imaginative and contented and in the process learned to concentrate, communicate better and integrate more into groups. In the States there have been similar findings on the negative effect of too much info. during the early years of childhood.

We persuade grandparents, aunts and uncles to give our children toys that require an imaginative input like lego, bricks, farm animals and especially good books. They still get too many toys so I box them up and bring them out gradually.

I gather that the National Consumer Council is trying to help young people to develop their own strategies for consumer education, building up young people's skills by working with their interests as consumers

Puberty, that potentially troubling, inevitable step into adulthood, love and the ability to reproduce and start a family oneself, is marred and masked by modern consumerism which finds yet another profitable market to exploit.

Sexuality is hived off from love and responsibility; lewd lyrics are thumped out over the air waves and near-pornographic images assault the newly-awakened sensuality with skimpy clothes – often made in sweat shops exploiting child labour in third world countries, and then sold to an unaware young public.

It is indeed a profitable market – intent on quickening mindless consumerism much in the manner of the earlier model of selling sweets and fizzy drinks to the very young; goodies that give a quick energy-rush before leaving it depleted and unfulfilled in terms of real nourishment.

This may all sound rather prudish but there is no doubting the cynical opportunism of marketeers to make the utmost profit out of a potential captive market. If only we as parents had the same dedication to the almost imperceptible stages of growth in our children and could target them with understanding and appropriate behaviour; to promote and allow positive development or unfurling of their natural talents – or perhaps that assiduous attention in itself, would also be a source of over-stimulation!

But "the unexamined life is not worth living" *(Socrates)* and certainly, to be aware of how much children are manipulated by big companies, who are disconnected from the idea of true value and whose main focus is economic profit, is no bad thing.

I've just read an article in a leading newspaper (pre-Christmas) that actually said that parents should order presents on the internet in good time otherwise they would have to face the 'recriminations' of their disappointed children!

We are managing to ward off the consumer, materialistic society. It is hard work but really rewarding.

I feel there is over-compensation in material things and it has become a vicious circle – mothers must work to afford all these additions as well as a higher standard of living. To me, it seems like being on a treadmill and whether it can ever be reversed is hard to forecast.

'Wipes'…children are always being cleaned! No mud, no germs… this is tied in with 'stranger danger' and means that a child is fearful of the world that they should be stepping into with confidence.

Regarding consumerism and materialism, children's overt expressions of this are (like their parent's issues of lack of attention span, addiction problems and workaholisms) connected to their earliest maternal deprivation.

I do not think there are any easy prescriptions. However, awareness is a very powerful thing and books and writings on this subject have a great effect. Many parents are uneasy about the lack of freedom in their children's lives and increasing awareness can only be good. But sometimes the same parents are happy with the demands for scholastic achievement based only on exams etc. as they have not questioned what society values themselves. I would very highly recommend a book called *Conscious Parenting* by Lee Lozowick. He writes brilliantly and concisely on subjects like TV, technology and our response to them when raising our children; it's the best I've read.

To minimise the harmful effects of materialism/consumerism/technology, I have:

a) limited the amount of TV (before he was two he almost never watched TV!).

b) restricted what he watches – just a few cartoons and nature programmes.

c) no computer access. I use my computer sometimes but he is not allowed to touch it.

d) computer games/technology games. I will keep these out of our house as long as I feasibly can. I doubt he will ever have a TV of his own until he can afford to buy one!

Already at under five, my children are being asked to lots of parties and I have to invite them all back. They expect their party bags to go home with. I quite enjoy packing them with silver paper coins, lollies that glow in the dark, chocolate animals, etc. but most people just order them all on the internet. I don't know how I can afford it when they are teenagers! Last birthday I gave them all a pot and a sunflower seed and that was a great success, but you have to go with the trends – like a treadmill.

I was a late mother with very few friends with babies. I remember holding a large party for my daughter when she was three. There were two children aged around six and eight who kept seeking me out before the end of the party telling me a few times "We are leaving now, thank you" or some such. I was left with a very pleasant feeling and thought what good manners they had, congratulating their parents on their charming offspring. It only occurred to me after my daughter had been invited to other parties, that perhaps they were expecting me to give them their party bags – a novelty to me. How green can you be?!

I felt it was easier to resist the consumerism when my children were small because we just didn't have the money and that was explained to them. Years ago I believe it was easier because there just was not the amount of material goods or convenience foods available anyway (early seventies). Even so, I can remember vividly the fights about buying 'sensible' Clarke's shoes!

I have been reading in *Finding Sanctuary* by Abbot Christopher Jamison, about the importance of silence – for children too. Thinking of the importance of silence and solitude, Jamison writes "To know yourself and to grow requires the insights that only solitude can provide". (It is also an antidote to our noisy environment – I notice noise pollution more and more.) I also read that there is a Quiet Garden movement founded by an Anglican Priest in 1992. Now there are Quiet Gardens all around the world!

The Quakers find a time for silence within their school day. At one school, no longer a Quaker establishment, they have retained this aspect with one minute's silence during lunch time or at the end of the morning assembly.

A child that is loved, encouraged, acknowledged and supported, grows up, hopefully, to do her best and maybe become a star, but the main thing is that she should be happy in whatever she is doing.

"Four angels round my bed, one to watch and one to pray, two to keep evil spirits far away"!

"All we are saying, is give peace a chance" *John Lennon*

Chapter 12
Controlling Our Time

"What is this life if full of care,
We have no time to stand and stare"
'Leisure' by W.H. Davies

There is a growing 'Slow' movement which began in Italy and now has international connections. The message is to take life more slowly and not be caught up in the vortex of speed which seems to be a characteristic of modern day living and where the children are swept along with the adults.

If we consider each of the chapters in this book dealing with young children's basic needs, it becomes evident that the time factor is all-important in dealing with them. Caught up in this whirlwind, children are all too happy to be like the adults and to grow up as quickly as they can.

The most precious thing about good family life is to be able to spend time together doing something that everyone enjoys. It might be a picnic in a spot where there is plenty for the children to do, an outing to the sea, or a popular film. It needs to be at a time when there are no pressures of work or school.

Children need a definite rhythm in their day to day lives. This gives them a sense of security; so meal-times and bed-times become assured, however much they may protest about the time to go to bed. There is so much they want to do: watch a programme, surf the internet, telephone, or of course, just play, and they just can't fit it all in.

Emotional needs require enough time to help resolve them; for example, it might be a case of bullying which must be nipped in the bud. It is not easy to get children's confidence so that they will tell you immediately if bullying is taking place. It is very much a case of being sure that they will be listened to, in a relaxed way; giving them your full attention.

Creative play is their 'work' for young children and this must not be hurried and squeezed in between other demands. When they have to do something else, like eat a meal or go shopping, they need plenty of warning to finish off and clear up. When the creative play is in a park or in the countryside, which gives full range to their activities, parents or carers have to take time to make the journey and then to watch over them at a safe distance as, although there can be over-reaction about child safety, they have to be safe-guarded in public or remote places. This kind of play calls for timelessness and privacy, which is so essential for the development of their imagination and creativity.

Closely linked to outdoor play is the importance of being in touch with nature, especially now that our planet is under such threat. This takes even more time as young children like to browse amongst flowers and watch all sorts of creatures. The very essence of nature is that it has its own pace and cannot be rushed. They have shown that they are soon old enough to care for the environment, whether by recycling or looking after wildlife. Older children can raise their voices along with adults to protect the planet. It is claimed that children as a whole are more conscious of the need for action than many adults and they can be all too aware of the lack of time; that urgent action is called for now.

The issue of having enough time is paramount in all children's physical development: time to have sufficient sleep; time to grow your own foodstuffs and cook them; time to enjoy the company of a family (without idealising every situation!). Of course home-cooking is time-consuming, but there are short cuts without destroying the food value and convenience foods can also be a time-saver, on occasion.

What about exercise? Walking is so essential that time should always be allowed for it, even if it is much quicker to go by car. And this will help protect the environment.

The whole education system is dominated by time. Even before they are drawn into the formal provision of nursery schooling, parents are made to feel that they cannot start too early to improve their infants' chance of getting a head start. From then on it is hurry all the way with tests and exams; a total of seventy by the time of A levels – and there are many casualties on this journey. The practice of dividing all subjects into little boxes creates a scramble to switch to the next lesson, especially in secondary schools, whereas the more holistic system practiced by schools following the philosophy of Rudolph Steiner and other innovative pioneers, can have a much more leisured and connected approach.

Time should be allowed for reflection on the learning process; time to assimilate and to connect with what is already known, so that it is not merely an accumulation of facts and information. This may be achieved by balancing the overcrowded curriculum with creative areas which are often neglected as they are frequently not included in the tightly loaded syllabus, and by facilitated discussion groups and even by guided fantasies and meditation. Time pressures on the teachers are reflected in the pupils and the parents and the end result for many children is to be turned off what should be a fulfilling and enjoyable experience.

With regard to behaviour, it takes time to deal with anti-social conduct in a way that will be meaningful. As has been discussed, many adults still favour some kind of physical punishment, which can be a quick slap and then the lesson has been taught and is over and done with, but is it? Children, especially young ones, need to go more deeply into their behaviour patterns with a growing awareness of their responsibilities towards others; similarly any resolution of conflictual situations often calls for long and careful negotiations until both parties are finally satisfied with the outcome. All of these approaches demand more time to be effectual.

It is obvious that the time factor dominates the use or misuse of all new technology: television, computer games, DVDs, mobile phones, the internet, etc. These are wonderful innovations and it is up to parents, in the first instance, to see that they do not take an undue amount of their children's precious time.

Finally, the adoption of values we want our children to embrace needs plenty of time for mutual contact and discussion, otherwise how can they be fully aware of and reflect our own value system? Otherwise they may become more conversant with the values reflected in the media, particularly television; for example, the aspiration to grow up quickly in order to become a star, or at least a celebrity, is a major feature of our competitive society.

There is another aspect of contemporary society that is intrinsically bound up with the need to go slow and take time. That is the great increase in noise levels in all walks of life. This makes it more important than ever that children (and grown-ups) have time to be still and quiet, perhaps in the form of meditation or just sitting still in a quiet place; the chance to have a breather.

It is when we take stock of the role of time in all of our lives that we realise how much we can become its slave. Have our natural time clocks become out of sync? We need to make sure that we give our children the precious gift of time to be themselves. We all have an internal clock. Recent research has shown that there is a part of our brain that regulates our sense of time and gives us a natural rhythm. One of the most revealing findings from research is that our internal clocks have speeded up since the industrial revolution. It is as though we are impelled to go faster, and of course our own behaviour is a model for that of our children.

The man who timed the expert bricklayer and then set the target for the workforce to follow suit was adopted by industrialists as a model to be imitated in all of their money-making enterprises and this set the pattern right up to modern day.

"To an adult used to making every second count, unstructured time looks like wasted time." Carl Honore, author of *In Praise of Slow (and stillness:* my addition to the title!).

Parents' contributions

With my new-born baby I had to slow down my life. Breast feeding was great for this. I had to sit down and relax and connect with my baby. I found it very therapeutic and as this is about childhood slowing down, this could be where we need to begin.

Spending time with each individual child doing something special – it could be a bike ride. No TV during the week.

I feel as a parent, it is important to remember that you are an individual also with your own needs and aspirations and that your children should learn to respect your time; if you have friends around, they cannot always be the centre of attention. Also when children have after-school activities, the parent should control what they themselves can manage to do without running themselves into the ground.

If there is one thing we must make time for, it is having family outings. We try to pick things that are free and where children are specially catered for like the art galleries and museums.

Do we expect too much of ourselves, too much of others, and, most importantly, too much of our children? This can create a gulf between where they think they are and where we believe they should be, so the present moment, the precious 'now', is overladen with pressure and anxiety, as if it is the wrong place to be instead of the best place to be.

Focusing on future goals, we lose the pleasure of the journey, always ahead of ourselves and never content. Sensitivity and awareness, with time for compassion, tolerance and understanding are replaced by the destructive force of meeting targets; no time for feelings, dreams and visions. Instead of celebrating individualities and difference the inability to conform is seen as failure. Yet failure only exists when performance is measured against unmet targets.

I feel that the most important thing you can give a child is time: time to explore the natural world in walks, being in gardens, looking at the wildlife, learning about the natural world around them first-hand, going to parks and woods, feeding ducks, at home – providing play-dough and toys to nurture imagination in play, painting, playing with jigsaws.

Consideration and mental and practical preparation for a radical change in your life really has to be the first step when considering having a child. It is not good enough to consider them as an accessory that can be fitted in to a busy schedule – another activity which denotes another successful enterprise – the family who can manage everything with a good work/play balance and an income from two wage earners who can afford the perks. We must be aware and beware the encroachment of business attitudes and economic goals that have crept in to child-rearing (even that word sounds like factory farming).

There has been much made of the idea of 'quality time' in recent years. Although this sounds perfectly commendable, on closer examination, it reflects an idea whereby time has to be divided into work and play. Also, that 'quality' comes only from special moments put aside outside of the daily living pattern. For a young child living in the moment can be full of quality for much of the time unless it has been taught to think in terms of nice and nasty. It is often the parents who consider daily living a chore and the child is then part of the chore and the problem.

Consider a busy working family. Shopping has to be done and these days, it will invariably involve a trip to the supermarket. Young children cannot be left alone at home. Shopping cannot always be done during school time if working. So, of course, the children come too which adds to the perceived chore. It will take much longer before you and the children can relax at home. But what happens at home? Do you then need to entertain them in some way? Why not consider the trip as play? Do not consider the time you can shop by yourself as the normal and therefore with children it becomes a rush. Allow more time and bring a bit of quality into the daily or weekly chore. a) Either teach them to shop with you. b) Choose a time which is relatively quiet (if possible) and enjoy them running up an empty aisle. c) Teach them to steer a trolley. (They will soon have bikes!). d) Give them some choice in what you choose. "What shall we have today darling, broccoli or spinach?" Basically give them time to play in this wonderful space and cornucopia of goodies – involve them in your life, your duties. It takes extra time in the beginning (back to the fundamental issue of time) but it will repay you later (when they can do your shopping). If they have played and enjoyed their time, they are likely to be less demanding on your return home. Don't give them payment or sweets for any job which make up the everyday needs of living.

Quality time can be had by letting your children play at being grown up – the parents allowing time to do a job with their child that normally takes them no time at all alone. Treat the child as your apprentice! Where possible involve them in decisions.

The idea of quality time so often is a marketing ploy – a trip to Alton Towers at a long awaited weekend when both parents are at home. Lots of money spent. But a long journey cooped up in a car with possible traffic jams and a late return is rarely a pleasure for children. Their bodies need to move, particularly young boys. Too much excitement or adrenalin in one lump is released during the visit. Parents may be exhausted on return with a week of work to look forward to. Children may be hyper and have homework to catch up on. It is a time-squeeze rather than a time-stretch. Consider whether young children would not have preferred a weekend at home doing something together – that is the important point: maybe washing the car but taking three hours with chat and a water fight: or building a bonfire or making a meal together: or go to a market together with few essentials to buy but a time to spend browsing. No travelling at all for a weekend can be a wonderful break in itself. Sharing space and time helps to produce quality. None of these activities involve the notion of going somewhere else or spending money. If it is only thought of in those terms, think again. When you are in love, it doesn't really matter where you are. Essentially make them part of the daily patterns, not a hived-off group that has completely different needs. Don't do all the work yourself because it is easier and faster. You will find it much more difficult to establish patterns later on if they are used to 'being served'.

You want to be a fulfilled mum and if you do have to go to work, usually because of needing the money or to pursue a career, you can experience the guilt of not giving the children what they need. The tide has changed from "I'm only a housewife". I think that time is probably one of the all-time pressures that they feel – "I'm not giving them the foundations they need". It is fighting against time, feeling that you will never be able to do as well as you want to be able to, trying to adapt from work to home, quality time, homework and meals that means everything gets less time.

Chapter 13
Parent Power in Action for Children

Be the change you want to see in others.
Mahatma Gandhi

Parents are beginning to realise something of their potential power; they are the chief body of customers, both as adults and providing for their children. The marketeers are fully aware of this and specially target the young so that they will get their parents to 'fork out'.

We are organised as a democracy, but we may feel that our small protest on behalf of our children has no effect in the great scheme of things. However manufacturers are much more sensitive about customers' wishes than we realise. So let us explore how parents, grandparents and everyone concerned about the unfulfilled needs of children can help to ensure they are better provided for.

Here are some ways in which they can use their power. For example, they can demand that their elected representatives give full support to the overall needs of families, and more importantly, that they carry out promises made during election time.

Parents can be under considerable stress these days and it is not a sign of failure on their part if they need support outside the family to help resolve pressing problems, especially on the emotional level. We do need greater provision of therapeutic help and we have to ask for it, both for our offspring and for ourselves.

National guidelines on how to deal with children's emotional problems, which can't be separated from our own, could also be invaluable. Similarly leaflets could be distributed by ante-natal clinics, nurseries and primary schools on the importance of talking to your child and, even more important, of listening to what they have to say.

Government and local authorities should provide many more facilities for children to play safely: for example, by employing carers in play areas and parks that are imaginatively designed for creative play and not restricted to unadventurous equipment because of stringent safety regulations. With regard to safety on the roads, parents could petition for bicycle lanes, lower speed limits, traffic-slowing humps and play streets in cul-de-sacs.

Intrinsically connected with the need for safe play is for children to be in touch with nature. Again, more safe provision in natural surroundings is vital for the child's well-being, let alone the fact that their generation will be the custodians of our planet. They must have safe access to as many green areas as possible, often achieved piecemeal through parents' action.

We cannot separate our children's need to be in touch with nature from the whole issue of protecting the environment. Much of this responsibility rests with government and local legislation but parents also have a responsibility to make sure this is carried out, explaining to their children the reasons why and involving them in any campaign where it is appropriate for their age-group if, of course, they want to.

The powers-that-be should have the responsibility to inform young parents about their children's physical needs, for example, guidelines on sleep, noise levels on personal stereos, healthy food and exercise. Again, this could be in the form of very simple leaflets distributed by GPs, clinics, nurseries and schools. These should be easy to read for busy parents and in addition to the more detailed pamphlets on special needs which are already available in baby clinics.

With regard to healthy food, schools should follow up the wonderful example of Jamie Oliver and money should be specially designated for adequate kitchen staff for good school-cooked lunches, with no packed lunch boxes allowed.

Plenty of exercise is necessary for a healthy body. Parents need to be vigilant that no more school playing fields are sold off and that barren, concrete playgrounds are converted into imaginative and natural areas for physical skill and games. They could also co-operate with teachers in making the case for body-friendly school furniture, which allows for good posture when in the classroom.

We are gradually ridding ourselves of the old antagonisms between parents and teachers, each blaming the other for any shortcomings. More than ever it is essential to have mutual respect and co-operation between them. Often parents feel inhibited about voicing their fears with regard to the preponderance of tests and exams, not realising that many, if not most, teachers feel the same. Together they will be more likely to influence government policy. There are many ways of giving a hand in the school's activities, for example, parent meetings, offering to help in the classroom and PTAs; the more contact there is, the more understanding that the mutual concern is for the well-being of the children and the greater likelihood there will be to engage in joint action.

With regard to behaviour, one can see a pattern that veers towards a punitive approach to any misbehaviour in our present society. Throughout this book, the emphasis has been on well-established boundaries with mutual respect and retribution following bad conduct, and zero tolerance of physical punishment. Again, on a national scale, parents could demand a more positive approach, rather than policies such as punishing parents for their children's disruptive or truanting conduct.

It is not only the family which needs to keep technology in

control, but also the companies owning television channels and websites, or producing software, mobile phones and computer games – and most especially the advertising agencies. The media could do a lot more in giving parenting advice on all aspects of children's needs, as they do in France and Australia, for example. Programmes should not be confined to extreme situations, where distraught parents have to call on specialists to instruct them how to deal with their out-of-control offspring. Parents need to be reassured that they are managing what is the most important job in the world. If their collective voice requesting programmes on parenting and child development proves successful, they will have more status and greater confidence that they are doing a good job. In the same way, parents need to be heard on any issue that they regard as essential for their children's well-being. One particularly worthwhile aim would be to ban advertising directed at children under the age of twelve. Sweden is an example of where this is the law.

Hurried childhood has permeated the whole of our society and, although how much slowing down is possible depends on the family, parents can very effectively use their consumer power to resist attempts to flood the market with expensive fashion clothes aimed at 'tweenagers' and younger children, which are inappropriate for their age group. They need to challenge the whole ethos of marketing, which is to achieve a high turnover of goods that rapidly become out-of-date or are so shoddy that they will be discarded for the latest new ones.

When parents challenge any aspect of our consumer society, they are also challenging the values which lie beneath it. So a protest about shoddy toys is one against the values of a throwaway society; likewise a plea for more green spaces is aimed at the value attached to preserving the environment.

These are just a few examples of how parents can make their views and sometimes their protests heard. Much depends on getting in touch with others who feel the same way and sometimes action can be taken together. This is not a plea for 'professional' parent protesters, but where there is an issue which people feel strongly and which affects their children, it is amazing what parents can accomplish.

Finally, we need to be watchdogs of the media for any decline in standards. For example, marketers should be banned from exhorting children to 'pester' their parents to buy items that they advertise, as should websites that promote the voyeurism of teenagers by encouraging them to video brutal bullying and gang violence and inviting viewers to add comments.

The TUCs general-secretary Brendan Barber said "Firms that have a healthy work/life balance are still very few and far between". Unsocial working hours means that many parents are at work when their children are at home and at home when their children are at school. Just 17 per cent of working parents have a nine to five, Monday to Friday job, with many working weekends. Child care is split between parents who sacrifice their time together and this can contribute to a breakdown in relationships. The Chief Executive of Working Families, Sarah Jackson, warned "For some families the time-squeeze is hurting emotional and physical wellbeing and stunting family development. Research has found that children in such families spend less time learning and more time alone." Campaigners argue that all parents should have the right to request flexible working hours and the right to request a limit to the amount of unsocial working hours.

Parents' contributions

In 2003, a panel of specialists from the Commission on Children at Risk recommended that 'authoritative communities' unite all groups in the community that serve children and young people to address concerns about childrens' deteriorating mental health. They should have an authoritative policy, respectful of children's and teenagers' point of view but also setting clear boundaries. Put authority figures in the places our kids want to play.

Call for a ban on all E numbers as additives – especially in sweets and soft drinks – they have been found to cause hyperactivity in children.

Join forces with other parents – there's safety in numbers.

Parents should stand up for their children if they think they are being bullied. Take action with the school in that respect.

Be prepared to challenge any authority, any person and any situation, if they feel their child is unhappy, victimised, being unfairly treated or treated in a way which is unacceptable to them as parents.

Parents must work together to lobby politicians, councillors and anyone who can wield power in support of children's well-being. They could make a big impact on the government and the purveyors of the media.

At a meeting of 'Growing Old Disgracefully' we went round the group to ask what change they would want in order to promote the well-being of young children in our present society. Their answers varied from smaller classes in school, better pay for teachers, organise family education, boost the morale of teachers by cutting down on SATs and abolishing the league tables, good after-school clubs, greater involvement in PTAs, more help to parents and recognition of the importance of parenting, monitoring excessive violence on TV and no advertising on children's television.

Appendix I

This is an example of how schooling could be a fulfilling and happy time.

Rudolf Steiner Education: The Steiner Waldorf Schools
by Richard House – Roehampton University and Norwich Steiner School

> *Receive the children with reverence;*
> *Educate them with love;*
> *Relinquish them in freedom.*
> Rudolf Steiner

In this book Mildred Masheder has referred throughout, either implicitly or explicitly, to *holistic* approaches to children's educational and childhood experience, and there are a number of educational approaches which strive to provide children with the kind of holistic, sometimes spiritually informed experience that Mildred Masheder clearly believes is essential for children's individual well-being in particular, and for the healthy evolution of humanity more generally. Without wishing to minimise the wonderful educational work done in such approaches as Montessori, human-scale education and the small-school movement, the open-school movement in the USA, the forest schools, and home educators the world over, perhaps the most well established and rapidly growing holistic educational approach in the world today is Steiner (Waldorf) education, and it is this approach on which I will be focusing in this appendix.

Rudolf Steiner (1861-1925)

It is something of an historical mystery as to why Rudolf Steiner's uniquely insightful contributions in so many diverse fields are still comparatively little recognised. Steiner's uncompromisingly *holistic* approach to human experience was many decades ahead of its time; and with his collected works numbering an extraordinary 350 volumes, his lasting legacy includes uniquely innovative 'impulses' in fields as wide-ranging as curative education and social therapy (the world-renowned Camphill Communities); biodynamic agriculture (precursor of organic agriculture); holistic (anthroposophical) medicine; architecture and design; the arts (Eurythmy, painting, speech and drama); organisational consultancy; ethical banking and finance (the Triodos Bank) – and, of course, education.

Rudolf Steiner founded the movement today still known as Anthroposophy, which is a spiritually informed yet scientific approach to understanding the world, and the place of the human being in the cosmos. Steiner was a relentless scourge of the one-sided materialism that prevailed in his day, and he brought a spiritually informed perspective to his educational worldview, which viewed the human being as far more than a material body.

In 1918 Steiner was asked to help found a school in Stuttgart, and in 1919 the first 'Free' Waldorf School was opened. Waldorf is today the world's largest and most rapidly growing independent schooling movement, represented in countries and continents the world over with almost 1,000 schools, some 1,600 Early Years settings and 60 Teacher Training centres worldwide. Steiner's educational works translated into English number approaching twenty volumes. Here, I can only present a bare summary of his educational approach; the interested reader can usefully start with the 'further reading' material listed at the end of this appendix.

Educational Philosophy

In Steiner's developmentally informed approach, the teacher's task is to provide the appropriate learning environment consistent with the needs of the unfolding child. This in turn requires the teacher's profound understanding of the developing human being, and a radical openness to experiencing the *being* of children in their totality; and much of Steiner's writings are taken up with a detailed articulation of such an understanding. There is a very 'modern' feel to this aspect of Steiner's approach, with the growing child's rhythm of development being broadly organised in archetypal seven-year phases which approximately correlate with the unfolding 'subtle bodies' of the developing child (namely, the physical, etheric and astral bodies, and the ego).

Between birth and seven, the child learns predominantly through imitation, repetition, movement, rhythmical activity, and free, unintruded-upon play; and her main task is the (unconscious) development of **the will** in an atmosphere of reverence, love, warmth, and care for the young child's developing senses. Then, from seven to fourteen, the child lives predominantly in **the feeling realm**, and learns through living pictures with an emphasis on beauty. From fourteen to twenty-one, the child comes into the realm of **ideas, thinking, and a deep desire for truth**. Within this overall schema, formal learning is avoided until the developmental marker of the change of teeth (at between six and seven years of age), and Steiner emphasised how the introduction of formal, abstract learning (e.g. reading and writing) before this age was positively harmful to the child – a finding which is beginning to be confirmed by modern research. This later introduction to formal schooling is routinely followed in much of continental Europe.

The Class Teacher And The Upper School

Between ages seven and fourteen, the Waldorf pupil ideally has the same class teacher, providing a continuity and 'intimacy of relationship' which is notably missing in the mainstream fragmented curriculum, and which, for Steiner, is profoundly nourishing for the growing child. Waldorf-educated pupils typically speak with glowing praise when recalling the formative influence of this class teacher relationship.

In the upper school from fourteen onwards, subject teaching predominates, but 'subjects' are taught in a 'trans-disciplinary' way which seeks to avoid the artificial disciplinary boundaries of conventional education. Thus, science is taught in a living, 'Goethean-observational' way which unites science with an artistic sensibility typically missing in conventional science teaching – as C.P Snow famously urged in arguing for reconciling the sciences and the arts. Modern technology and science are arguably in urgent need of an artistic and even spiritual sensibility, and Waldorf is possibly unique in offering this.

There is little competitive testing and examinations in Waldorf education, with empowering *formative assessment* approaches strongly favoured. Yet Waldorf pupils typically obtain public examination results considerably better than the national average, despite not being 'taught to the test' for these examinations. Moreover, many Waldorf-educated pupils go on to university and have highly successful academic, professional or artistic careers; and university admission systems are now beginning to recognise the unique qualities of Waldorf-educated children, thereby easing their access into higher education.

Aspects of Waldorf Pedagogy

The holistic approach in Waldorf education means that teaching is always done *from the whole to the part* – providing an antidote to the mechanistic reductionism of the 'modernist' worldview still so prevalent in today's troubled world, and manifesting so damagingly through the 'audit culture' in mainstream education. The holistic notions of 'emotional intelligence' (Dan Goleman) and 'spiritual intelligence' (Dinah Zohar) were also quite explicitly prefigured by Steiner, critical as he was of the *Zeitgeist*'s one-sided intellectualism.

Waldorf education is very practical, with as much emphasis being placed on creative, craft and manual activity as on intellectual pursuits. For Steiner, the healthy pursuit of the former can only enrich and deepen the latter – holism again. Relatedly, education is seen as a living creative *art* rather than as a programmatic science, with *human relationship* being an absolutely central aspect of any educational experience. The teacher's *being-qualities* are therefore seen as being more important than the amount of factual information that the teacher imparts. The teacher's *personal development* is therefore a crucial aspect of being a Waldorf teacher.

These are just some of the so-called 'intangibles' of effective teaching, which Steiner repeatedly emphasised, and which a mechanistically 'positivistic' approach to teaching undervalues or completely ignores. Steiner sees education at its best as an intrinsically *healing force* for the child.

School Organisation

Waldorf schools have a 'flat', non-hierarchical structure, with no headmaster/mistress, and with a College of Teachers which works consensually to decide matters of school policy, administration, etc. – a truly radical social innovation in Steiner's time. Freedom is, therefore, a central aspect of Waldorf education, enabling young people to enter the world as independent, creative thinkers, free of the quasi-authoritarian ideology that arguably dominates much conventional schooling.

A Very Modern Education...

Waldorf education has much to contribute to current educational debates. Steiner's notion of the 'threefold social order' transcends both capitalism and socialism, and he tirelessly argued against the state having any direct input into the educational sphere – a view gaining far wider currency in the light of the stultifyingly toxic 'audit-culture' mentality now engulfing state education.

The 'death of childhood' is also a motif increasingly echoing throughout modern culture, and Steiner was a fierce defender of the right to a childhood relatively unburdened by misguided 'adult-centric' and technocratic agendas.

Rudolf Steiner's educational philosophy and Waldorf praxis together provide an impressively coherent 'post-modern', 'new paradigm' antidote to the worst excesses of an ecologically unsustainable materialistic *Zeitgeist*; and in this sense it is supremely relevant as we struggle through the death throes of 'modernity' and towards a new post-materialistic age.

Further Reading

Dorothy Male, *The Parent and Child Group Handbook: A Steiner/Waldorf Approach*, Hawthorn Press, Stroud, 2006

Brien Masters, *Adventures in Steiner Education: An Introduction to the Waldorf Approach*, Rudolph Steiner Press, London, 2005

Lynne Oldfield, *Free to Learn: Introducing Steiner Waldorf Early Childhood Education*, Hawthorn Press, London, 2003

For further information and resources, contact the *Steiner Waldorf Schools Fellowship*, Kidbrooke Park, Forest Row, East Sussex RH18 5JA, England
Phone: +44 (0)1342–822115 Fax: +44 (0)1342–826004
E-mail: mail@swsf.org.uk
Web site: http://www.steinerwaldorf.org.uk/

Dr Richard House is a Senior Lecturer in Psychotherapy and Counselling at Roehampton University, London, and works part-time in Norwich Steiner School, which he has helped to found. He co-initiated (with Sue Palmer) the 'toxic childhood' and 'play' Open Letters published in the *Daily Telegraph* in September 2006 and 2007 respectively, to both of which Mildred Masheder was a signatory.

Appendix II

Bravo for Jamie Oliver for his 'Healthy School Dinners Campaign'. It shows how pressure on governments can be successful, even if there is still a long way to go. School dinners should be firmly in the hands of the school with enough government financial backing. Parents need to push constantly for one cooked meal per day for their children.

When I open kids' lunch boxes I find that in the average primary school, some 80 per cent contain food that is inappropriate while I would say that some 20 per cent is mildly dangerous. A healthy lunch box should contain: a starchy food like wholemeal bread, potatoes, cereal, rice, etc; a protein food for growth: meat, oily fish, eggs, cheese, beans, peas, nuts: fruit and vegetables for essential nutrients: dairy food to provide calcium for bones and a drink for hydration and additional nutrients: water, milk or pure fruit juice.

Jamie Oliver gives advice to parents: involve children in planning and shopping for food; offer small tasty portions of new foods; don't force children to eat food, simply provide healthier choices and other options: be a role model for healthier eating – if they see you enjoying salad and fruit and drinking water, they will too. He adds four easy changes: fresh fruit instead of chocolate; wholemeal bread instead of white; yoghurt instead of crisps. Variety is the spice of a lunchbox. He forecasts: 'The minute the parents all get together, something magic will happen.'

Appendix III

CHARTER FOR CHILDHOOD by the Alliance for Childhood

We, the undersigned representatives of organizations working in the children and parenting fields, teachers and members of the wider children's workforce, health professionals, campaigners, academics, politicians and individuals believe:

Marketing has laid roots in every aspect of children's lives, dictating how they play and learn and what they eat. This commercialization has become a barrier to a good childhood.

Engulfed with images of how they should look and be and what they should own, children are struggling to keep up, resulting in increasing rates of stress, depression and low self-esteem. In promoting a link between possessions, social status and self worth, marketing worsens the lived experience of poverty for children who cannot access lifestyles advertised to them and makes them prone to bullying if they have the 'wrong' clothes or toys or other goods. Marketing is exploiting too the increasing sexualisation of young girls in the name of profit. The relentless targeting of children by marketers selling foods high in fat, salt and sugar is contributing to all-time high levels of obesity and related health problems in children.

Concurrently there has been a steady decline over recent years in the opportunities children have for healthy outdoor play, as public spaces have become increasingly dominated by commerce and traffic, and children's leisure time has become increasingly fair game for market forces, on the whole promoting sedentary, screen-based pursuits.

This is a worrying and growing concern for parents, carers, teachers and children and urgent steps must be taken to help children rebalance their lives. We must, both directly ourselves and through our elected government, support children, parents, carers and teachers to withstand the pressures of commercialization and restore children's right to free play within the public realm.

Aims and Objectives of the Alliance for Childhood

Support family life.
The activities of the alliance promote and support family life, in all its forms, so that children grow up and develop in a secure and stable home environment.

Promote a developmentally appropriate' Early Years' curriculum.
Creative play and self-directed activities give children a sound basis for life-long learning and promote healthy emotional and social growth.

Work for better physical and emotional health for children.
Parents, educators and health care professionals can optimise their support for children by collaborating with each other and sharing their experiences.

Fight poverty and neglect in all forms.
Many children suffer poverty, neglect, abuse and discrimination, undermining the basic human right to a nurtured childhood.

Question the role of electronic media in child development.
Over-exposure to television, computers and video games adversely affects children's physical, emotional, social and mental development. By sharing experiences, parents and educators can work together to offer children a creative and healthy balance.

Highlight the dangers of commercialism aimed at children.
Children need to be protected from the manipulation of hard-selling advertising until they are mature enough to make informed choices.

Improve childcare facilities.

Parents need affordable, high quality childcare, providing a caring environment with appropriate activities for each child's developmental needs.

To this end, we call for:

A: Protecting children from advertising

1.1 A ban on all advertising to children under seven years old, in both broadcast and non-broadcast media, including in-store marketing to children by way of displays, shop layouts and packaging.
1.2 A ban on product placement in all children's TV programmes and films.
1.3 The introduction of a watershed of 9 p.m. for television advertising of all foods high in fat, salt and sugar (HFSS foods) and support for Baroness Thornton's Private Members Bill seeking to legislate for this.
1.4 The introduction of a statutory Standards code in advertising to seven to sixteen year olds carrying a legal requirement to comply.
1.5 Provision of support to parents, carers and teachers and accessible resources to help them understand the impact of commercialisation on children and suggest ways they can offset it, for example ways of helping children understand the media.

B: Providing opportunities for all children to participate in outdoor play.

2.1 The recognition of children's play provision as essential.
2.2 The strengthening of flexible working arrangements for all parents and carers, to enable them to spend more time with their children.
2.3 The inclusion of play provision in the 'core offer' prospectus

for extended services.

2.4 The inclusion of quality outdoor play space in guidance for Building Schools for the Future (BSF) tenders and in all new schools and childcare provision proposals.

2.5 The recognition of playwork as a key part of the children's professional workforce.

2.6 The introduction of performance indicators for local authorities on the extent and the quality of outdoor play provision for local children.

2.7 The inclusion of space for outdoor play in planning frameworks for all new housing builds and re-designs.

2.8 A reduction of the speed limit to 20 m.p.h. or less in all residential areas, more Home Zones and improvements in street design to create child-friendly neighbourhoods.

2.9 The creation of a new funding stream for play provision to secure investment above and beyond lottery funding.

Appendix IV

Open Letter to the Daily Telegraph, September 2006

This is an article based on this letter which was signed by 110 teachers, psychologists, early childhood specialists and children's authors who have called on the government to prevent the continual erosion of creative childhood.

British children are being "poisoned" by a culture of processed food, computer games and over-competitive education, a group of academics and authors claimed today.

The authors of the letter – who include children's writers Philip Pullman and Jacqueline Wilson, the former children's laureate Michael Morpurgo and the director of the Royal Institution, Baroness Greenfield – warn that children need to develop as human beings.

"Since children's brains are still developing, they cannot adjust as full-grown adults can, to the effects of ever more rapid technological and cultural change," the letter says.

"They still need what developing human beings have always needed, including real food (as opposed to 'junk'), real play (as opposed to sedentary, screen-based entertainment), first-hand experience of the world they live in and regular interaction with the real-life significant adults in their lives," they write.

The experts condemn Britain's increasingly "target-driven" education system and urge the government to recognise children's need for more time and space to develop, demanding an urgent public debate on child rearing in the 21st century.

"They also need time. In a fast-moving, hyper-competitive culture, today's children are expected to cope with an ever earlier start to formal schoolwork and an overly academic test-driven primary curriculum," they say.

Mr Morpurgo said there was a "drip, drip, drip effect" of academic pressure and marketing which was killing childhood.

"It's gradually soaking like a poison into the culture," he said. "There is less room for reading, for dreaming, for music, for drama, for art, and simply for playing."

The letter was circulated by Sue Palmer, an ex-head teacher and author of the book *Toxic Childhood*, and Richard House, a senior lecturer at the research centre for therapeutic education at Roehampton University in London.

"Children's development is being drastically affected by the kind of world they are brought up in," Ms Palmer told the *Daily Telegraph*. "It is shocking." "A child's physical and psychological growth cannot be accelerated. It changes in biological time, not at electrical speed. Childhood is not a race."

Bibliography

Adams, John, 1979, *Games Children Play around the World*, Toys Ltd

Alliance for Childhood, 2004, *Tech Tonic*.

Antidote, 2003, *The Emotional Literacy Handbook*, David Fulton. www.fultonpublishers.co.uk and www.antidote.org.uk

Axeline, Virginia, 1969, *Dibs in Search of Self*, Ballantine Books.

Beaver, Diana, 1997, *Easy Being: Making Life as Simple and as Much Fun As Possible*, Useful Book Company, UK.

Berrien Berends, P, 1983 *Whole Child/Whole Parent*, Harper & Row.

Bettelheim, B, 1987, *A Good Enough Parent*, Pan.

-1995, *A Good Enough Parent: Guide to Raising Your Child*, Thames & Hudson.

Biddulph, Steve, 1998, *Raising Boys: Why Boys are Different and How to Help Them Become Happy and Well-balanced Men*, Harper Collins.

Blishen, E, (ed), 1969, *The School That I'd Like*, Penguin.

Britton, J, 1972, *Education Towards Freedom*, Pelican Books.

Brooks, Jane B, 1994, *Parenting in the 90s*, Mayfield Publishing Company, Mountain View, USA.

Bruner, Jerome S, 1966, *Towards a Theory of Instruction*, Norton.

-1964, *On Knowing. Essays for the left hand*, Harvard University Press.

1983, *Under Five in Britain*, Blackwell.

Buckman, P, 1973, (ed), *Education Without Schools*, Souvenir Press, London.

Buckton, Chris, 1980, *The Experience of Parenthood*, Longman.

Burke, C & Grosvenor, I, 2003, *The School that I'd Like*, Routledge Falmer.

Burns, Sally & Lamont, Georgeanne, 1995, *Values and Visions,* Hodder & Stoughton, London.
Carey, D & Large, J, 1982, *Festivals, Family and Food,* Hawthorn Press, Stroud.
Children of the World, 1994, *Dear World: How Children Around the World Feel About the Environment,* Bodley Head Children's Books.
Children of the World, 1994, *Rescue Mission: Planet Earth,* Peace Child International; Kingfisher Books, London.
Citizen Foundation, 2002, *Young Citizen's Passport,* Hodder and Stoughton, London.
Coplen, D, 1982, *Parenting,* Floris Books, Edinburgh.
Crowe, B, 1986, *Play is a Feeling,* Unwin.
Day, Jennifer, 1997, *Children Believe Everything You Say,* Element Books, Shaftesbury, Dorset.
De Bono, Edward, 1983, *The Mechanism of Mind,* Penguin, Harmondsworth.
Doing Things in and about the House. 1983, Photographs and Activities about Work, Play and Equality, Serawood House.
Donaldson, Margeret, 1992, *Human Minds: an Exploration,* Allen Lane, London.
Elkind, David, 1981, *The Hurried Child; Growing Up Too Fast Too Soon.* Addison-Wesley Pub. Co. and 2001, Da Capo Press.
Faber Adel & Mazlish, Elaine, 1980, *How to Talk so Kids Will Listen & So Kids Will Talk,* Avon Books, New York and !995, *How to Talk So Kids Will Learn at Home and in School,* Scribner
Farrington, Lorna, 2002, *Changing our School, Incentive Plus,* PO Box 5220, Great Horwood, Milton Keynes, MK17 0YN.
Gardner, Howard, 1999, *Intelligence Reframed. Multiple Intelligences for the 21st Century,* Basic Books, New York.
Goleman, Daniel, 1996, *Emotional intelligence. Why it can matter more than IQ: Emotions,* Bloomsbury, London. and 1997, *Emotional Intelligence.* Bantam Books,

Goodman, P, 1971, *Compulsory Miseducation*, Penguin, London.
Greenfield, Susan, 2003, *Tomorrow's People: How 21st Century Technology is Changing the Way we Think and Feel*, Allen Lane
Haim, Ginott, 1969, *Between Parent and Child*, Avon Books, New York.
Haller, I, 1987, *How Children Play*, Floris Books, Edinburgh.
Hawkes, Neil, 1996, *School Policy*, West Kidlington Primary and Nursery Schools, Oxford.
Healy Jane M, 1990, *Endangered Minds – Why Children Don't Think- and What We Can Do About It*, Simon & Schuster.
Herschkowitz MD, Norbert & Chapman Herschkowitz, Elinore, 2002, *A Good Start in Life: Understanding Your Child's Brain and Behaviour From Birth to Age 6*, Dana Press.
Holford, Patrick, 2004, *Patrick Holford's New Optimum Nutrition Bible*, Piatkus Books Ltd.
Holt, J, 1970, *How Children Learn*, Penguin, London.
Honore, Carl, 2004, *In Praise of Slow: How a Worldwide Movement is Challenging the Cult of Speed*, Orion Books
Human Values Foundation, 1994, *Education in Human Values: Lesson Plans 1-3 Truth, Love, Peace,*
 -1994, *Education in Human Values Foundation,*
 -1994, *Education in Human Values: Manual,*Human Values Foundation, Ilminster, Devon, UK
Judson, S, 1983, *A Manual on Non-violence and Children*, New Society Publishers.
Knight, M, et al, 1982, *Teaching Children to Love Themselves*, Spectrum.
Kreidler, W, 1984, *Creative Conflict Resolution*, Scott Foreman
 -1990, *Teaching Concepts of Peace and Conflict*, Educators for Social Responsibility, Cambridge, MA, USA.
Large, M, 1990, *Who's Bringing Them Up?* Hawthorn Press, Stroud.
Leach, Penelope 2004, *'Your Baby and Child'* Penguin

Lindstrom, Martin, (with Seybold, Patricia B.), 2003, *BRANDchild* (revised edition) Kogan Page Limited.
Linn, Susan, 2005, *Consuming Kids: the Hostile Takeover of Childhood*, New Press.
Livingstone, Tessa, 2005, *Child of Our Time; How to Achieve the Best for Your Child from Conception to 5 Years*, Bantam Press.
Louv, Richard, 2005, *Last Child in the Woods: Saving our Kids From Nature-Deficit Disorder*, Algonquin Books.
Martin, Paul, 2005, *Making Happy People: the Nature of Happiness and its Origins in Childhood*, Fourth Estate.
Masheder, Mildred, 1989, *Let's Play Together*, Green Print, London.
-1990, *Windows to Nature*, World Wide Fund for Nature.
-1994, *Let's Enjoy Nature*, Green Print, London.
-1997, 3rd Edition, *Let's Co-operate*, Green Print, London.
-2004, *Positive Childhood: Educating Young Citizens*, Merlin Press, London
-2007, *Carrier's Cart to Oxford*, The Wychwood Press, Oxford.
-1989, Video *Let's Co-operate – Illustrative Co-operative and Parachute Games*, 75 Belsize Lane, London NW3 5AU
Mayo, Ed, 2005, *Shopping Generation*, National Consumer Council.
McLuhan, Marshal & Fiore, Quentin, 2001, *The Medium is the Massage*, Gingko Press.
McNeal, James U, 1992, *Kids as Customers: a Handbook of Marketing To Children*, Lexington Books.
Miller, A, 1987, *For Your Own Good*, Virago, London.
Montessori, M, 1969, *The Absorbent Mind*, Del, New York.
Mosley, Jenny, 1993, *Turn Your School Around; a Circle Time Approach to the Development of Self-Esteem*, L.D.A, Chris Lloyd Sales & Marketing Service UK.
Mosley, Jenny & Sonnet, Helen, 2002, *Games for Self-Esteem*, L.D.A.

Neuberger, Julia, 2005, 2005, *The Moral State We're In: a Manifesto for a 21st Century Society*, Harper Collins.

Noel, Brook, 1990, *Back to Basics: 101 Ideas for Strengthening Our Children and Our Families*, Champion Press Ltd.

Orrey, Jeanette, 2005, *The Dinner Lady: Change the Way Your Children Eat, for Life*, Bantam Press.

Parentline Plus, 1999 *Being a Parent*, Hawthorn Press.

Peachey, J Lorne, 1981, *How to Teach Peace to Children*, Herald Press.

Piaget, Jean, 1962, *Play, Dream and Initiation in Childhood*, Norton, New York.

Pinker, Susan, *The Sexual Paradox*, Atlantic Books

Postman, N & Weingartner, C, 1971, *Teaching as a Subversive Activity*, Penguin, Harmondsworth.

Postman, Neil, 1985, *Amusing Ourselves to Death*, Random House.

 -1994, *The Disappearance of Childhood*, Vintage.

Provenzo, E F, 1991, *Video Kids: Making Sense of Nintendo*, Harvard University Press, Cambridge, Mass.

Prutzerman, P, et al, 1978, *The Friendly Classroom for a Small Planet*, Avery Publishing Group.

Richardson, Alex, 2006, *They Are What You Feed Them*, Harper Collins.

Rogers, C, 1983, *Freedom to Learn for the 80s*

 -1985, *Freedom to Learn*, Charles E Merrill.

Russell, B, 1926, *On Education*, Allen & Unwin.

Satter, Ellyn, 2000, *Child of Mine: Feeding With Love and Good Sense*, Bull Publishing Company.

Schor, Juliet B, 2004, *Born to Buy*, Scribner.

Sigman, Aric, 2005, *Remotely Controlled: How Television is Damaging our Lives and What We Can Do About it*, Vermilion.

Skynner, R & Cleese, J, 1983, *Families and How to Survive Them*, Methuen, London.

Storr, Anthony, 1992, *Music and the Mind*, Harper Collins, London.

United Nations: 1892 *The Universal Declaration of Human Rights – An Adaptation for Children*, UN Publications, New York.

Walker, P & F, 1988, *Natural Parenting*, Bloomsbury, 1987 and Interlink, NY.

Warnock, Mary, 1998, *An Intelligent Person's Guide to Ethics*, Duckworth, London.

Weare, Katherine, 2000, *Promoting mental, emotional and social health; a whole school approach*, Routledge, London.

Whitaker, Patrick, 1993, *Practical Communication Skills in Schools*, Longman, Harlow.

Whittingstall, Jane, 2005, *The Good Granny Guide*, Short Books.

Williams, Rowan, 2000, *Lost Icons; Reflections on Cultural Bereavement*, T & T Clark, Edinburgh.

Williams, Rowan, 2003, Tuesday, 23 July pp. 2-4, *Article* in The Times.

Winnicott, D, 1964, *The Child, the Family and the Outside World*, Penguin, Harmondsworth.

Woodhouse, Sarah, 2003, *Sound Sleep: Calming and Helping Your Baby or Child to Sleep*, Hawthorn Press.

Woolfson, Dr Richard C, 2002, *Small Talk: From First Gestures to Simple Sentences*, Hamlyn.

Also by Mildred Masheder:

Positive Childhood
Educating Young Citizens
A resource book for teachers and parents of primary school age children.
'A welcome reminder of our responsibilities here, and a stimulus to thought and action.' Dr Rowan Williams, Archbishop of Canterbury.
1854250949 £9.99

Let's Play Together
An Exciting collection of over 300 games and sports which put co-operation before competition – and make everyone a winner! You'll find traditional party games, circle games, musical, board and guessing games, games for the lively and energetic, for the drama-minded or the artistic, nature games, and parachute games.
Playing games will never be the same again!
1854250132 £8.99

Let's Co-operate
This book contains many ideas for parents and teachers to share with their children. With sections on: a positive self-concept, creativity, communication, co-operation, getting on with others and peaceful conflict resolution. Illustrated with photographs and drawings.
1854250906 £7.99

Let's Co-operate Video
A lively and colourful video which illustrates many of the games in Let's Play Together and explores parachute games.
£9.99

Let's Enjoy Nature

A book to help parents, teachers and their children get in touch with nature and care for the planet.
With over 500 ideas for activities including: making things from nature; conducting experiments; growing plants; nature games; seasonal celebrations; exploring the countryside; conservation in the home and beyond. With 150 illustrations.
1854250922 £8.99

Freedom from Bullying
This is a practical book designed to help teachers and parents work with children to prevent bullying at school from nursery to secondary stage, and deal with it when it occurs.
Conclusive evidence shows that co-operation between parents, teachers and children can free a majority of pupils from a scourge that has plagued countless generations.
1854250922 £8.99

All available from Mildred Masheder at the address below or from good bookshops (except the video).

Mildred Masheder, 75 Belsize Lane, London NW3 5AU
Tel. 020 7435 2182
Visit the Merlin Press/Green Print web site:
www.merlinpress.co.uk

Organisations

Antidote, 45 Beech Street, Barbican, London EC2Y 8AD
Association for Citizenship Teaching, www.teachingcitizenship.org.uk
Learning through Landscapes, 3rd Floor, Southside Offices, The Law Courts, Winchester, SO23 9DL, schoolgrounds-uk@ntl.org.uk and www.ltl.org.uk
Living Values, Brahma Kumaris, 3 Fullamoor Cottages, Clifton Hampden, OX14 3DD. www.bkpublications.com
Sapere, Dialogue Works, Northmead House, Puriton, Somerset TA7 8DD
The British Wheel of Yoga, 25 Jermyn Street, Sleaford, Lincs NG34 7RU
The Circle Works, 6 Temple Yard, Temple Street, Bethnal Green, London E2 6Q
Mediation UK, Alexander House, Telephone Avenue, Bristol BS1 4BS